PRINCIPLES OF
MARKETING

CLEP* Study Guide

WITHDRAWN

© 2012 Breely Crush Publishing, LLC

*CLEP is a registered trademark of the College Entrance Examination Board which does not endorse this book.

971123011143

Published by Breely Crush Publishing, LLC
10808 River Front Parkway
South Jordan, UT 84095
www.breelycrushpublishing.com

ISBN-10: 1-61433-025-5
ISBN-13: 978-1-61433-025-7

Printed and bound in the United States of America.

*CLEP is a registered trademark of the College Entrance Examination Board which does not endorse this book.

Table of Contents

The Marketing Concepts – An Overview 1
    Section 1: What is Marketing? 1
    Section 2: Marketing System 3
The Marketing Opportunities – An Analysis 5
    Section 1: The Marketing Environment 5
    Section 2: Consumer Market and an Analysis of Buyer Behavior 7
    Section 3: Organizational, Reseller and Government Markets 16
Organizing for Marketing Efforts 18
    Section 1: Basic Objectives and Strategies 18
    Section 2: Marketing Organization 23
    Section 3: Types of Planning in Marketing 24
Planning and Marketing Mix 26
    Section 1: Types of Products and Product Traits 26
    Section 2: The Product Mix Decisions 27
    Section 3: Channels of Distribution 30
    Section 4: Product Promotion Efforts 34
    Section 5: Advertising 36
    Section 6: Price Determination 37
    Section 6: Marketing Effort Control 40
Writing a Marketing Plan 41
Legal Aspects of Marketing 42
    Legislation 42
    Taxes 43
Sample Test Questions 44
Test Taking Strategies 75
What Your Score Means 75
Test Preparation 76
Legal Note 76
References 77

The Marketing Concepts – An Overview

SECTION 1: WHAT IS MARKETING?

In layman's language "market" generally means a place where sellers and buyers meet to exchange what they have in excess for what they require. Sellers sell products for money and buyers buy products in exchange for their money.

Marketing is highly influenced by change. Change in any area of buyer's lives can influence the way they spend money. Some types of changes which have to be taken into consideration are social, economic, technological, political and legal changes.

Social changes are changes which relate to behavior and lifestyle. For example, changes in fashion are considered social changes. Another factor to consider would be the age structure of a population. Analyzing these factors (and changes in them) can give a company a sense of what the market will be like in the future.

Changes in the economy also have a large effect on buying patterns. In a bad economy, people are less likely to spend money and most business suffer. On the other hand, when the economy is doing well, all businesses benefit. Changes in inflation, interest rates and average wages are also economic changes.

Technological changes are also important. Increased internet usage affects marketing strategy, advancements in consumer technology create new and ever changing products and new production technology allows products to be made and shipped faster and cheaper. Technology affects all levels of marketing. This makes keeping up with the changes an important element of marketing.

Political changes can affect international trade. For example, the creation of the European Union opened up trade among all European nations. For the United States, politics relating to Middle Eastern countries has a significant affect on gas prices.

Legal changes also have potential to affect marketing. In the early 1900s, the antitrust movement completely changed the way businesses operated. Today, laws regarding environmental issues, consumer protection, labor and other factors regulate how businesses are allowed to market and function.

Marketing: This can be defined as a set of activities undertaken by human beings aimed at promoting and completing exchanges.

Marketing Management – a definition: The core concept behind marketing has to do with exchange. Marketing Management, therefore, is the analysis, ideation, planning, organizing, executing and controlling of stated targets with pre-identified audiences for mutual gain. To get an effective response, an Optimal Marketing Decision Variables is arrived at, which works as a blueprint for success.

SALES AND MARKETING CONCEPTS:

SALES: aims to achieve:

| Increased Sales Volumes and Good Profits | through | Hard Sell and Promotion | of | PRODUCTS |

MARKETING: aims to achieve:

| Profits through Customer Satisfaction | through | Integrated Marketing | of | What the Customer wants |

An Integrated Marketing Approach always works in terms of the customer's needs, desires and wants and places them above company needs. Let us see where a Marketing Department lies in an organizational setup and with what authority structures.

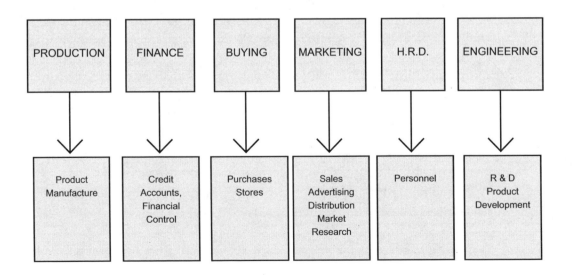

SECTION 2: MARKETING SYSTEM

In a basic model, a company dispatches goods and services to the market, together with communication, and in exchange receives money value (Dollars) for the goods plus information. But today's marketing system has become more complex and sophisticated. Today's marketing system is given in a schematic diagram for easy understanding:

INNER CORE

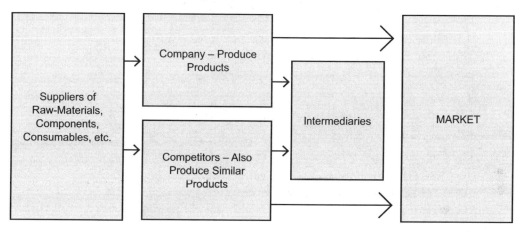

This is the inner core of today's marketing system. This, of course, is enveloped by an outer core, which is as important as the inner core.

OUTER CORE

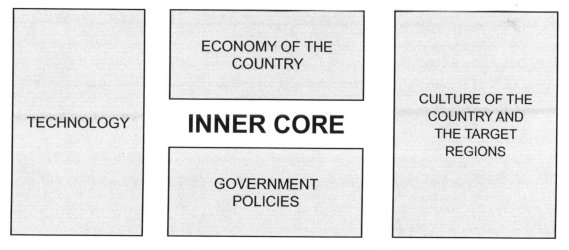

If technology is fast changing, the marketing effort will be affected. Likewise, if the economy is bad, it may tell upon marketing your product. Government policies have a major say in your marketing. Good business-friendly policies will encourage you into putting more effort in marketing. The culture of the country, as well as the region where your target market is situated, will also have a role to play. In the USA, beef eating is common and plenty of beef is consumed daily. But in India, where the Hindu culture demands abstinence from consuming beef, marketing beef products would take a unique approach.

Demand Variables: These are causes that have the potential to negatively affect the sales of a company or the entire industry. Example: A car company's sales are affected by the people's attitude towards cars, disposable income, infrastructure facilities and the general conditions of roads, the cost of petrol/diesel as the case may be, the total of high as well as upper middle class groups within the country, competitors and their strategies in terms of price, terms of payment, special product features and promotional activities. Demand variables are grouped into: (1) Customer variables (a) number of people in the market, and, (b) the rate of product usage. (2) Environmental variables – these are the outer core we have seen earlier. (3) Competitive variables – causes that are influenced by competitors and have a role in affecting your sales, and, (4) Marketing decision variables – these are causes that the company possesses to influence sales.

Marketing Decision Variables: In any company's marketing program, it is the Marketing Decision Variables that are bound to play a very important role. The best classification of marketing decision variables was given by E. Jerome McCarthy – the "Four P's" – (1) Product (2) Place (3) Promotion and (4) Price.

Marketing Mix: It is the most important task of the Marketing Department to find out the optimum setting for its Marketing Decision Variables. This Optimum Setting is considered the Marketing Mix of the company.

Marketing Effort: Refers to a company's employment of inputs, such as men, material and money, into the company's overall marketing process in order to generate sales.

Marketing Allocation: It refers to a company's allocation of total marketing efforts to its various products, different customer segments, different salesmen and different sales divisions.

Marketing Strategy: It refers to a company's overall objectives, tactics, policies and guidelines that govern over a period of that company's marketing effort.

The strategy spells out the total allocation, the ideal mix required and the level of marketing efforts needed to achieve a predetermined target. Environmental changes and the level of competitive thrust determine the overall strategy.

Market Response: It relates to the response in the pattern of sales to the marketing effort.

The Marketing Opportunities – An Analysis

SECTION 1: THE MARKETING ENVIRONMENT

An organization dealing in the marketing of products works in a complicated and fast-changing marketing environment. Constant vigil to identify impending changes and swift adaptation to such changes allows an organization to survive and better still, prosper. A marketing environment consists of a number of tiers. They are (1) the organization of a corporate environment, (2) the market environment, and (3) the macro environment. An organization and its Macro Environment together form an Ecosystem. Turbulence in the ecosystem either creates threats or opportunities to organizations depending upon their attitude.

THE TIERS OF A PRODUCTS MARKETING ENVIRONMENT

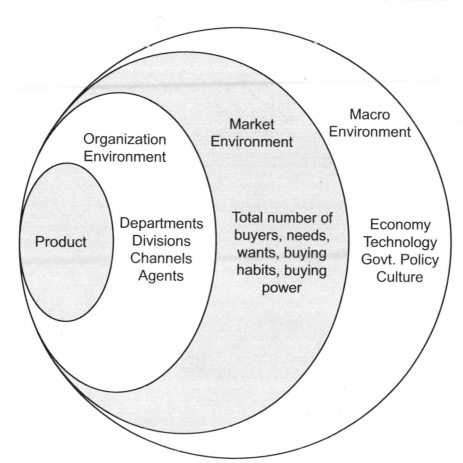

Organization Environment

Market Environment

Macro Environment

Product

Departments Divisions Channels Agents

Total number of buyers, needs, wants, buying habits, buying power

Economy Technology Govt. Policy Culture

The marketing macro-environment is very important, and therefore, let us study the four factors of which it is composed. The economic environment symbolizes the rising income of persons, and as a corollary, the changing patterns of retailing, wholesaling and physical distribution. The technological factor indicates the speed with which products become obsolete on account of technological innovations, and increased R&D expenses on account of the company's quest to find a more stable product. The Government policy factor compels you to constantly and consistently look for policy changes and adapt to new policies. The culture factor ensures safe life and that long perceived and followed beliefs are not impaired. Of these four factors let us study in detail the Economy factor, which is vital for many decisions a company has to make as it impacts the market. Cyclical changes in the economy's overall level of business are known as the business cycle. There are four stages in any business cycle:

(1) Prosperity (also known as boom)

(2) Recession (it is a slow down of business)

(3) Depression (gloom, also called bust stage)

(4) Recovery (the economic upswing)

Why do swings take place? It is because of variations in the demand and supply continuum for goods, the volume of consumer spending, level of employment, the consumers' ability (that is, level of disposable income), interest rates, Government Tax policy and spending. If there is a huge demand, the business invests in more machinery and plants to meet such increases.

Inflation: This refers to a decline in purchasing power due to price levels rising faster than income. This can happen at any stage of the business cycle.

THE COMPETITIVE ENVIRONMENT AND THE MARKET STRUCTURE

All producers and marketing organizations vie for the general customers' purchasing power. The competitive environment is governed by the market structure within which it operates. In market structure there are four basic types:

1. Pure Competition – many small sellers and many small buyers; none of them individually can effect any changes on demand and supply.

2. Monopolistic Competition – many sellers and many buyers but their products have subtle or vast differentiation from the others.

3. Oligopoly – a few large sellers account for the major portion of total industry sales – Branding with unique selling propositions helps.

4. Pure Monopoly – this is just the reverse of pure competition. Large public sector units dominate the industry. Literally no competition is allowed.

SECTION 2: CONSUMER MARKET AND AN ANALYSIS OF BUYER BEHAVIOR

Today all markets are complex and unique. To understand the essentials of markets, a marketing system needs a general framework, which tries to understand the market's composition, character, needs and wants. There are four questions that will give an insight into this system.

1.   What did the market use to buy? This gives you an insight into the <u>objects</u> of purchase.

2.   Why buy? This gives an insight into the <u>objectives</u> of such purchases.

3.   Who is buying? This gives an insight into the <u>organization</u> for such purchases.

4.   How does it buy? This gives an insight into the general <u>working of the organization</u> that effects purchasing.

THE 4 – P'S OR THE COMPONENTS OF MARKETING DECISION VARIABLES:

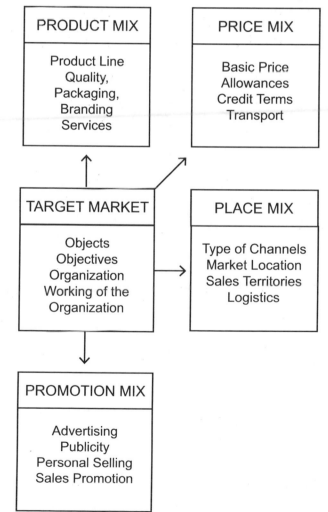

According to the specific characteristics of individual markets, the 4-P's of Marketing Decision variables are set. In a market where price is most sensitive, the organization tries to maintain the existing price levels even if a price increase from the organization's point of view is justified; it may offer more liberal credit terms or allow some allowances on the basis of more off-take, etc.

Consumer Markets: It is a market where product and services are purchased or hired solely for non-business (personal) consumption. The purchases are made by individuals or households. In the USA consumer markets are huge catering to more than 300 million individuals and families who consume products and services worth many trillions of US Dollars. Marketing people have recognized the existence of different groups and sub-groups within a given market and have developed strategies to cater to each group by developing products and services most suited to their varying needs. They segregate sub groups like (1) Men (2) Women (3) Children (4) Youth, and (5) Elderly – and offer differentiated products to suit the individual consumer of each such sub group. Having said that, it is better now for us to postulate a basis for the classification or grouping of a huge number of consumer products so we can get an insight into underlying marketing differences and implications on the Marketing Mix front.

Generally speaking, products can be classified as either industrial or consumer. The main differences between the two are in their purpose and who buys them. Consumer products are bought by individuals for personal or household use. They are typically purchased in retail stores. Industrial products are meant to be bought by companies and used to produce other products. For example, industrial products include raw materials like steel and iron or machines used in making products. Sometimes products can be either consumer or industrial based on what they are bought for. For example, a person buys a five pound bag of flour because they are making cookies. This is a consumer good. However, a pastry making company may buy ten thousand pounds of flour to mass produce pastries. In this case, flour is an industrial good.

DURABLE GOODS – NON-DURABLE GOODS AND SERVICES

Durable Goods: These tangible goods (actual goods), once bought, will satisfy you for many years (Example: Air Conditioners, Refrigerators, Clothing, etc.).

Non-Durable Goods: These are also tangible goods, which once bought may be consumed in a very short period of time (Example: Toothpaste, Soap, Ham, Biscuits, etc.).

Services: These are non-tangible activities, benefits and satisfactions that are offered by individuals with expertise (Example: Tailoring, Hair dressing, Cleaning, General Repairing, etc.).

The general characteristics in relation to marketing of durable, non-durable and services are:

<u>Durable goods</u> – Needs more personal selling, more seller guarantees and to charge a higher margin.

<u>Non-durable goods and services</u> – To develop loyalty over time, marketed in a number of locations, charging a small margin. Any marketing strategy should be tailored to meet these general characteristics.

Another classification based on consumer's purchasing habits gives us 3 different groups of goods:

1. <u>Convenient Goods</u>: Goods bought by consumers most often with relative speed without spending time on comparison (Example: Newspapers, soaps, detergents, tobacco products, etc.).

2. <u>Shopping Goods</u>: Goods bought by consumers after spending time considering its utility, value, quality, suitability, style and of course, price (Example: Cars, home appliances, dress materials, furniture, etc.).

3. <u>Specialty Goods</u>: Goods bought by consumers that have characteristics perceived to be unique and/or having good brand identification (Example: Branded goods, fancy goods, electronic goods, photographic equipment, etc.).

Another way that products can be classified is as heterogeneous or homogeneous. Homogeneous products are manufactured to be all the same. For example, a bread company wants all of their bread to be the same and a nail company wants every nail to be the same. In each case if there were an inconsistent or wrong item the company would receive complaints. However, other industries want to have diverse or varied products. In this case the products would be called heterogeneous. For example, donut shops have many different types of donuts to please as many people as possible. Another comparison would be the different between buying a pair of jeans at the store and going to a tailor. The jeans at the store are meant to be uniform, whereas the tailor will make custom goods.

CONSUMER BEHAVIOR

What are the objectives or goals a consumer while effecting a purchase is looking for? To put it simply, he is looking for a perceived need satisfaction. Needs are unlimited.

Maslow's Hierarchy of Needs

Maslow's Hierarchy of Needs consists of the following stages from the top down:

- Self Actualization
- Esteem Needs
- Belonging and Love
- Safety
- Physical Needs

These stages begin at the physical needs. First you need to have food, water, and shelter before you can worry about other requirements. Once those needs are met you may start to think of other necessities, such as safety. You might buy a gun or move to a more prosperous and safe area. Once you are fed, clothed and safe you will want to meet needs of belonging and love through relationships. If you feel loved, you may begin to think about your self-esteem and how you feel as a person, what you are contributing. The final stage, self-actualization, you may never meet. Most people do not.

A Buyer's buying decisions are generally influenced by the Buyer's cultural, social, personal and psychological factors. We will presently see all those factors that influence Buyer behavior.

FACTORS INFLUENCING BUYER BEHAVIOR

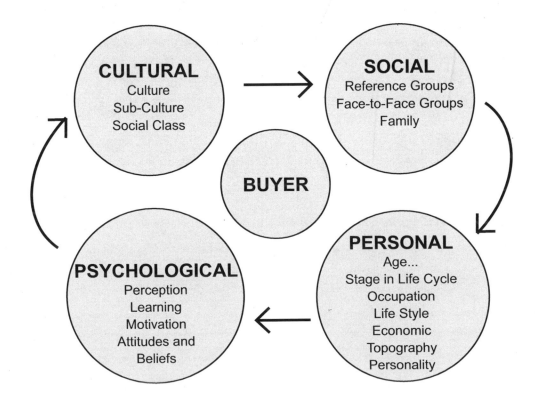

CULTURAL FACTORS

Culture: It is the most rudimentary determinant of a person's needs and wants and the resultant behavior. As we grow, we acquire a set of values, perceptions, preferences, attitudes and behavior through social interactions. Knowledge about products and other utilities are naturally culture specific.

Sub-culture: Every culture has within itself sub-cultures. These sub-cultures provide identity to its members. Sub-cultures are grouped as:

1. Nationality Groups – Americans, Chinese, English, etc.
2. Religious Groups – Christians, Muslims, Hindus, Jews, Buddhists, etc.
3. Racial Groups – Whites, Blacks, Orientals, etc.
4. Geographical Area Groups – North American, South American, etc.

These sub-cultures condition certain cultural preferences and prohibitions fashioning clear styles and attitudes. These factors have a say in clothing preferences, food choices, career ambitions and even recreation.

Discretionary income: Income that is left over after a person has paid for basic necessities, such as food, clothing, housing, and savings. This is money that they have to spend however they want (at their own discretion). The general equation is discretionary income=disposable income-savings-cost of living expenses. Disposable income is a person's net income after taxes have been paid. For example, a person makes $1,000 in a month. That month they have to pay $200 of it to taxes, $500 rent and $150 for other cost of living expenses. This makes their discretionary income $1,000-$200-$500-$150 or $150.

Social Class: Social stratification is a well known phenomenon. (1) Caste – aspirations of members is largely in keeping with the known and traditionally followed systems and practices. (2) Social Class – identifies members on the basis of (superior or inferior) positions held by them. Value orientation, education, income, occupation and net worth define a member of any stratified social class. Each social class has distinctive product and service preferences unique to them.

PERCEIVED MAJOR SOCIAL CLASSES[1]

1. **Upper Uppers:** Upper uppers are the social elite who live on inherited wealth and have well known families. They maintain more than one home and send their children to the best schools. They are in the market for jewelry, antiques, homes and foreign vacations. While small as a group they serve as a representative group for others to the extent that their consumption decisions are imitated by other social classes. They do not believe in ostentatious or showy lifestyles.

2. **Lower Uppers:** Lower uppers are persons who have earned high income or wealth through exceptional ability in their profession or business. They usually come from the middle class. They tend to be active in social and civic affairs and seek to buy the symbols of social status for themselves and their children, such as expensive cars, homes, and schooling. They include the nouveaux riches, whose pattern of conspicuous consumption is designed to impress those below them. Their ambition is to be accepted in the upper-upper status, a status that is more likely to be achieved by their children than themselves.

3. **Upper Middles:** Upper middles possess neither family status nor unusual wealth. They are primarily concerned with "career." They have attained positions as professionals, independent business persons, and corporate managers. They believe in education and want their children to develop professional or administration skills so that they won't drop into a lower stratum. Members of this class like to deal in ideas and "high culture." They are highly civic-minded and they are the quality marker for good clothes, homes, furniture and appliances and entertainment.

4. **Middle Class:** The middle class are average-paid white and blue collar workers who live on "the better side of town" and try to do the proper things; often they buy popular products to "keep up with the trends." The middle class believes in spending more money on "worthwhile experiences" for their children and aiming them towards professional college education. Better living means "a better home in a nice locality" with good schools.

5. **Working Class:** Working class consists of average pay blue collar workers and those who lead a "working class lifestyle," whatever income, school or job they have. The working class depends heavily on relatives for economic and emotional support, for tips on job opportunities, advice on purchase, and for assistance in times of trouble. The working class maintains sharp sex-role division and stereotyping. They tend to have larger families than the higher classes.

6. **Upper Lowers:** Upper lowers are working, although their living standard is just above poverty. They perform unskilled work and are poorly paid; often they are educationally deficient. Although they fall near the poverty line they manage to "present a picture of self-discipline" and "maintain some effort at cleanliness."

7. **Lower Lowers:** Lower lowers are visibly poverty stricken, and usually out of work. Some are not interested in finding permanent jobs and most are dependent on charity for income. Their homes, clothes and possessions are "dirty," "raggedy" and "broken-down."

SOCIAL FACTORS:

Reference Groups: A person may not be a member of such groups but identifies with it and aspires to become one – such groups are known as Reference groups. Example: A young boy adoring Michael Jordan and aspiring to become like him in Basketball, or a young girl adoring Sharon Stone and aspiring to become a star like her in Moviedom. Such persons subconsciously watch and mimic their Hero's attitudes and behavioral patterns. Such persons are influenced in the buying behavior too by their subject of adoration!

Face to face groups: These are groups which have direct and immediate influence on a person's opinions, likes and dislikes. Example: The person's family, friends, neighbors, peers, etc.

Family: A person's basic attitudes, behaviors and beliefs are developed during the formative years, formed through interaction with his family, which plays a most enduring role in such attitude formation. One's immediate family constitutes the most influential primary reference group. There are products with which different family members have a dominant role to play.

	Products	Dominant Member
1)	Television, Cell phones, Automobiles, Insurance, Air Conditioners, etc.	Husband
2)	Food items, Kitchenware, Appliances, Refrigerators, Washing Machines, etc.	Wife
3)	House, External Entertainment, Vacation and Traveling, etc.	Both Husband and Wife

Personal Factors: A person's age, state at which he is in the lifecycle, economic background, occupation, lifestyle, disposable income at his command, etc., all influence his buying behavior.

Psychological Factors: A person's needs and wants are unlimited. A specific need at a specified point of time takes precedence over others. There are (1) biogenic and (2) psychogenic needs. (1) The biogenic needs are concerned with your physiological state. Example: hunger, thirst, discomfort, etc. (2) Psychogenic needs arise on account of a person's specific need satisfaction relating to his psychological state of mind, which normally is not apparent. Example: satisfying the need for recognition, esteem, etc. In other words, biogenic needs refer to Maslow's physiological and safety needs while psychogenic needs refer to social, esteem and self-actualization need structures.

In psychological terms, cognitive dissonance is when a person feels and recognizes a discomfort due to conflicting ideas. In marketing, this emerges as buyer's remorse. Buyer's remorse (or cognitive dissonance) is when a person has second thoughts about whether they purchased the correct product. For example, a person may see a commercial for a product and be completely convinced that it is the best and immediately buy it. Later they see a commercial for a different brand of that product and are convinced that they have chosen wrong. They will then feel conflict. Either it will lead them to switch products, or they will decide that the commercial is wrong. Cognitive dissonance can also emerge after someone buys a large, expensive product, like a car. They may have really wanted the car when they bought it, but later realize that it was a little out of their price range.

THE CONCEPT OF FAMILY LIFECYCLE

There are seven stages in the lifecycle of a family and any buying activity is closely connected to the specific stage of the family life cycle present at that point of time.[2]

Bachelor stage: young, single people - Few financial burdens. Fashion opinion leaders. Recreation-oriented. Buy: basic kitchen equipment, basic not living at home. Furniture, cars, equipment for the mating game, vacations.

Newly married couples: young, no children – Better off financially than they will be in the near future. Highest purchase rate and highest average purchase of durables. Buy cars, refrigerators, stoves, sensible and durable furniture, and vacations.

Full nest I: youngest under six – Home purchasing at peak; liquid assets low. Dissatisfied with financial position and amount of money saved. Interested in new products. Buy washers, dryers, TV, baby food, baby medicines, dolls, and toys.

Full nest II: youngest child six or over – Financial position better. Some wives work. Less influenced by advertising. Buy larger-sized packages, multiple-unit deals. Buy many foods, cleaning materials, bicycles, music lessons, and pianos.

Full nest III: older couples with dependent children – Financial position still better. More wives work. Some children get jobs. Hard to influence with advertising. High average purchase of durables. Buy new, more tasteful furniture, auto travel, unnecessary appliances, boats, dental services, and magazines.

Empty nest I: Older couples, no children living with them, head in labor force – Home ownership at peak. Most satisfied with financial position and money saved. Interested in travel, recreation, and self-education. Make gifts and contributions. Not interested in new products. Buy vacations, luxuries, and home improvements.

Empty nest II: Older married couples, no children living at home, head retired – Drastic cut in income. Keep home. Buy medical appliances, medical-care products that aid health, sleep and digestion.

In addition to the family lifecycle, there are instances where a household will fall into one of the following situations:

Solitary survivor, in labor force – Income still good but likely to sell home.

Solitary survivor, retired – Same medical and product needs as other retired group, drastic cut in income. Special need for affection, attention and security.

BUYING ROLES

INITIATOR	The person who thought about it
INFLUENCER	His words influence the final act of buying
DECIDER	Ultimate decider of what, how, when and where to buy or defer decision
PURCHASER	Who actually buys
USER	Consumes or uses the goods purchased

There are five stages in any buying process. They are:

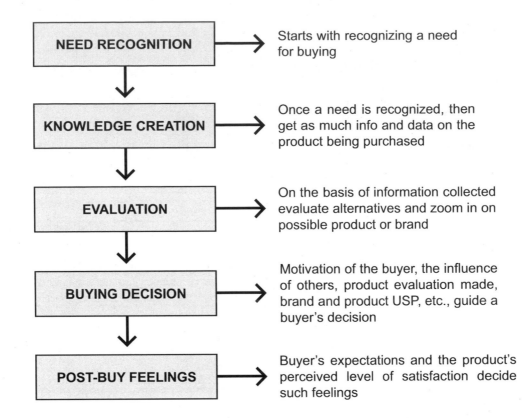

NEED RECOGNITION	Starts with recognizing a need for buying
KNOWLEDGE CREATION	Once a need is recognized, then get as much info and data on the product being purchased
EVALUATION	On the basis of information collected evaluate alternatives and zoom in on possible product or brand
BUYING DECISION	Motivation of the buyer, the influence of others, product evaluation made, brand and product USP, etc., guide a buyer's decision
POST-BUY FEELINGS	Buyer's expectations and the product's perceived level of satisfaction decide such feelings

SECTION 3: ORGANIZATIONAL, RESELLER AND GOVERNMENT MARKETS

ORGANIZATIONAL OR PRODUCER OR INDUSTRIAL MARKETS

The Organizational or Producer or Industrial Market is made up of business units that are engrossed in the manufacture of goods and services for sale or rental to other units. There are markets for raw materials, sub assemblies, manufactured materials and parts, equipment, installations, accessories, services, etc. The Organizational buyer is interested in bottom lines unlike consumers who are interested in need satisfaction. They are extremely skilled buyers and know the markets thoroughly. Geographically they are concentrated, unlike a consumer buying process where a central person, though influenced by other members, makes the final decision. In Industrial or Production or Organizational buying, the buying process is carried out by several knowledgeable persons participating in it. A consumer buyer can have choices – like ordering a BigMac or plain sandwich. An organizational buyer has no choices. If only carbon steel is required for a manufacture, he has to get only carbon steel and not bronze. He is not interested in personal satisfaction like a consumer buyer because he is purchasing a product for further production of another product. The demand for organizational or industrial or producer's goods, therefore, is <u>derived</u> and not <u>primary</u>. Industrial goods are purchased by trained professionals, known as purchasing agents or buying agents. Another important characteristic of industrial goods is that the demand is mostly inelastic, i.e., it is not affected by any change in price. However, the degree of demand is largely related to the condition of the economy. In a boom period where consumers purchase products frequently and consistently, it is bound to affect supply, and therefore, the producers start purchasing more production machinery and raw materials to augment supplies so as to meet the consumers' increased demand. The increase in consumer demand generates a multiplier effect on the producer's goods. They purchase much more than required to meet the increased consumer demand.

Reseller Market: This market consists of individuals and organizations such as agents, selling intermediaries, distributors, wholesalers or dealers, who purchase goods with the sole intention of reselling or renting them to others in the market and achieving a good profit margin. Resellers handle a vast variety of goods for sale. A reseller faces such questions as (1) What assortment to carry in stock (2) Who the vendor should be (3) What price, and (4) What terms? Any wholesaler or retailer can opt for any one of the four assortment strategies.

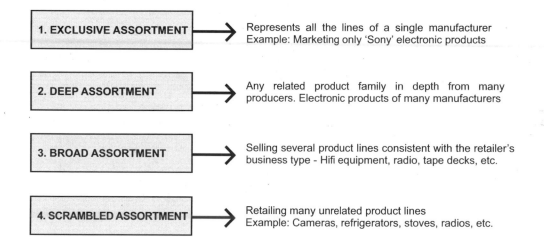

Reseller and the buying decision: Whether to involve in reselling activity of a new product or stay away depends upon the degree of profit the new product generates for the reseller. The greater the profit, the faster the involvement. Of course, the advertising backup, favorable credit terms and product utility are also taken into account. For an existing product, a reseller normally orders for stock when his inventory touches the reorder point.

The Government Markets: This comprises public sector undertakings that buy or rent goods for carrying out certain main functions of government, such as Federal, State, and Local governments, etc. Governments' buying is very huge. They buy from stationery to nuke materials and other items of warfare! Government buying procedures are highly specialized and in some cases cumbersome. Open bidding and negotiated contracts are employed in government buying. For standard items open bidding procedure is used. The accredited government agency invites bids from qualified suppliers for very well specified items. The supplier who has quoted the lowest price is awarded the contract.

Organizing for Marketing Efforts

SECTION 1: BASIC OBJECTIVES AND STRATEGIES

Demand Measurement: Success requires hard work. A company, if it wants to be very successful, must be able to measure the actual size of the market as of today and at a given future date. Quantitative Measurements are necessary to quantify an achievable target for the present year and for future years.

Market Demand: What is it? If you want to evaluate the Market Demand for a <u>product</u>, you have to take into account the <u>total volume</u> that you estimate to be bought by a predefined <u>target audience</u> in a given <u>geographical area</u> in a stated <u>time frame</u> within a given <u>marketing environment</u> covered by a clearly stated <u>marketing program</u>.

Market Forecast: The total market demand is likely to be in line with the marketing effort that a company is expected to put forth and this market demand that is assumed to be achieved is known as Market Forecast. The Market Forecast tells us the anticipated level of Market Demand for an anticipated degree of Marketing effort, happening in a given environment.

The Company Forecast: Every company anticipates a certain level of sales, during a given time period. It assumes what the marketing environment during that time period would be and it opts for a well thought out Marketing plan to achieve such anticipated sales. This, in essence, is the company forecast. In other words, it is a company's planned, targeted sales for its products during a given time period. The plan assumes that there won't be any drastic changes in the environment.

Sales Quota: It is some sort of a sales goal for each salesman, each product of the product line, all company zones or regions or divisions, each distributor and each agent. It is a managerial tool for stimulating sales.

Sales Budget: It is a cautious estimate of sales during a given period based on the overall sales forecast meant mainly to arrive at the anticipated level of purchases, the level of production of each product and to help cash flow decisions.

Methods of Estimating – Current Demand: How to estimate current sales potential? There are two methods: (1) The breakdown method, and (2) The buildup method.

1. The Breakdown Method: The production and sales of any company is finally linked to the Economic Environment of a country. If the Economic Environment is good, it reflects on the production and sales levels of products – there is a boom everywhere. On the contrary if the Economic Environment of a country is really bad, again it reflects in the business gloom and there is a reduction in output and consequent dip in sales. The Economic Forecast of a country is the index as to whether the business should increase or decrease sales. A marketing company gets hold of the economic forecast for the next fiscal time period and estimates the level of sales potential on the basis of the economic forecast. The GNP forecast is broken down into Division, Distributor, Retailer, Salesmen and products sales.

2. The Buildup Method: It estimates the total number of units of all products marketed by the company which a typical buyer in a given sales territory during a given period is likely to purchase among various competing products. The number arrived at then is multiplied by the number of potential purchases in that particular territory. This procedure is followed for all territories of the company and the individual figure of each territory is totaled up to arrive at the anticipated market potential.

Methods of Estimating Future Demand: There are a number of methods and a company uses one or a combination of more than one such method to arrive at the future demand. The forecasting methods normally used to determine future demand are: surveys of what the buyer intends to buy, estimate of salesmen, expert opinions, conducting a market test for the product to solicit indications of future response of the purchaser, Statistical Demand Analysis and, of course, Time Series Analysis. Whether it is estimating current demand or future trends, care should be taken to collect pertinent data and information in an authentic manner.

Market Segmentation: No two people think alike. Likewise, no market is full of people who think alike, act alike, or buy alike. Tastes differ between individuals. All markets therefore are heterogeneous. A given product may be liked in one particular market and may not be selling in another. Even in a market where it sells well, there may be pockets where it sells extremely well and pockets where there may be not much sales. Marketing organizations with a view to overcome such shortcomings segment markets on a number of characteristics. The idea is to subdivide a market into homogenous subsets of customers. Any subset or a number of such subsets may be taken in as a target audience in that market and approached with a specific marketing mix. This is the underlying principle of segmentation. Let us learn about segmentations;

SEGMENTATION VARIABLES:

Geographic	Demographic	Psychographic	Benefit
Nation – Region State – Areas City Climate/Terrain Population Density Density of the Market	Sex, Age, Amount of disposable income Spending Pattern Education Occupation Nationality Family	Social Class Lifestyle Personality Status Seekers Plain	Brand Loyalty Benefits Sought

There are other types of segmentations such as volume segmentation, marketing factor segmentation and product space segmentation.

STRATEGIES TOWARDS MARKET SEGMENTATION:

There are different strategies available to a marketing company towards Market segmentation:

1. Undifferentiated Marketing:
Only one product offered to hook all buyers. There may be only one Marketing Program.

Undifferentiated Marketing

2. Differentiated Marketing:
Separate products & separate marketing plan for individual segments.

Differentiated Marketing

3. Concentrated Marketing:
Selects beneficial pockets of one or more segments and market, concentrating all the company's effort there. Instead of looking for a small share of a large market, opt for a large share of one or a few submarkets.

Concentrated Marketing

One aspect of marketing is how to consider the market. Often, products will have a target group, or segment, which can be classified through demographic, geographic, psychographic or behavioral characteristics.

Demographics is the study of populations, and therefore demographic segments are related to classifications of people within a population. This includes people with similar age, family situation, ethnicity, gender, jobs, income, religion or a number of other factors. For example, a children's pool is more applicable to families then it is to the market as a whole.

Geographic segmentation is segmentation based on location. This includes what part of the country a person is from, urban versus rural areas, and similarly sized metropolitan areas. For example, a snow shovel company would do better off advertising to northern states with lots of snow than it would to southern states with little snow.

Psychographic segments are segments with similar lifestyles. These are groups of people with similar activities, values, interests, personalities and opinions. For example, marketing guns or cooking supplies at trade shows geared to that sort of product. This way, the people who are most likely to purchase or want the product have the most access to it.

Behavioral segmentation is based on people's attitude toward the product. For example, if the person uses the product often, occasionally or rarely. This type of segmentation also plays off of brand loyalty and nearby occasions (if it's close to Christmas or Father's day).

ORGANIZATIONAL OBJECTIVES AND STRATEGIES

Developing clear company objectives precedes a company's marketing planning. The objectives should spell out well thought out growth and competitive strategy. There are:
(1) Prime objectives (to aim for a stated end result high profit)
(2) Instrumental objectives (more basic aims to be accomplished – products, sales territories, salesmen, marketing instruments, etc.)
(3) Specific objectives (specific as to magnitude and time, average profit of about 15% over next 5 years, etc).

An organizational objective identifies employees with the organizational growth by providing a sense of purpose and work satisfaction. A well thought out objective may look like, "…to manufacture quality products that have the inherent characteristics for total customer satisfaction, provide a reasonable profit margin and aim for a greater market share…"

Robert Weinberg has the following basic strategic trade-offs each organization has to face:

1. Short term profits vs. long term profits
2. Profit margin vs. competitive position
3. Direct sales effort vs. market development effort
4. Penetration of existing markets vs. the development of new markets
5. Related vs. non-related new opportunities as a source of long term growth
6. Profit vs. non-profit goals (social responsibilities)
7. Growth vs. stability
8. No risk environment vs. high risk environment

Objectives are a sort of statement of intent on where an organization would like to be, whereas strategies are grand designs aimed solely at getting the organization there.

1. <u>Market Penetration</u>: the company seeks increased sales for its present products in its present markets through more aggressive promotion and distribution.

2. <u>Market Development</u>: the company seeks increased sales by taking its present products into new markets.

3. <u>Product Development</u>: the company seeks increased sales by developing improved products for its present markets.

4. <u>Diversification</u>: the company seeks increased sales by developing new products for new markets. This is not an intensive strategy.

SECTION 2: MARKETING ORGANIZATION

Every business unit has a variety of complex tasks to be performed and therefore requires men, machines, materials, money, and of course data and info. Marketing, in a basic setup, is all about order generation. The supply tasks are something like this in a basic setup.

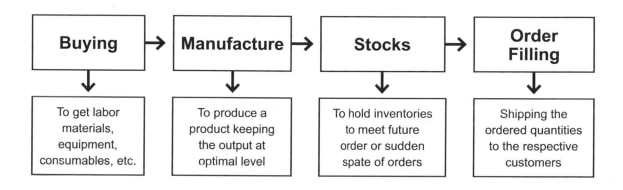

A function-oriented marketing organization will look like:

A product-oriented marketing organization will look like:

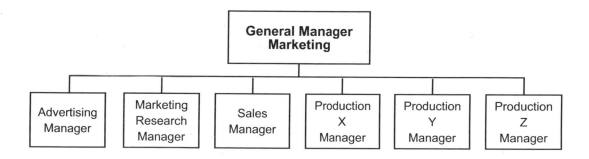

A centralized marketing organization will look like:

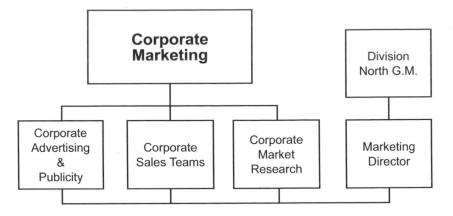

In decentralized marketing organizations, other than corporate marketing – corporate advertisement – corporate marketing research, which are common, the North Division will have General Manager, Marketing Manager and North's separate advertisement and sales team plus marketing research. They, of course, work within the overall corporate parameter set by corporate marketing.

SECTION 3: TYPES OF PLANNING IN MARKETING

What is planning? To put it simply, it is deciding <u>today</u> what you should do <u>tomorrow</u>. Planning is deciding at the present moment to achieve a stated objective in a predetermined future spelling out in clear terms how to go about it. How and where to start? It is better to study what Philip Kotler, the undisputed marketing guru has said in his epoch of a book, "…Marketing Management – Analysis, Planning and Control…"

"…Diagnosis: where is the company now, and why?
　　Prognosis: where is the company headed?
　　Objectives: where should the company be headed?
　　Strategy: what is the best way to get there?
　　Tactics: what specific actions should be undertaken, by whom and when?
　　　　Control: what measures should be watched to indicate whether the company is succeeding?..."

The above questions lead you to the present state of affairs of the company, where is it heading, actually where you want it to go, how to get there, what are the tactics and who will ensure that the company is on the right track.

TYPES OF PLANNING IN MARKETING

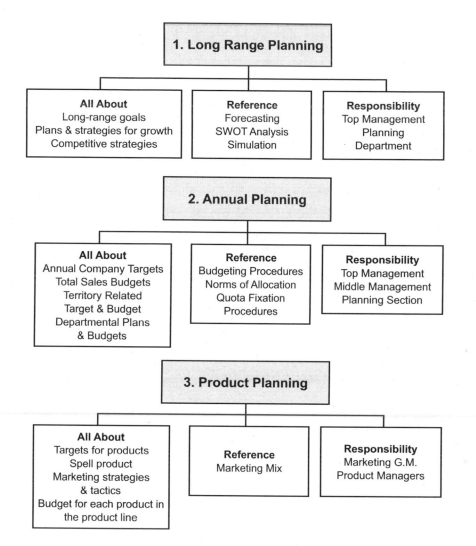

1. Long Range Planning

All About	**Reference**	**Responsibility**
Long-range goals	Forecasting	Top Management
Plans & strategies for growth	SWOT Analysis	Planning
Competitive strategies	Simulation	Department

2. Annual Planning

All About	**Reference**	**Responsibility**
Annual Company Targets	Budgeting Procedures	Top Management
Total Sales Budgets	Norms of Allocation	Middle Management
Territory Related	Quota Fixation	Planning Section
Target & Budget	Procedures	
Departmental Plans		
& Budgets		

3. Product Planning

All About	**Reference**	**Responsibility**
Targets for products	Marketing Mix	Marketing G.M.
Spell product		Product Managers
Marketing strategies		
& tactics		
Budget for each product in		
the product line		

SWOT ANALYSIS

SWOT Analysis is a very important part of marketing. SWOT is a way to identify your strengths and weaknesses. SWOT stands for:

- Strengths
    - What are your advantages?
    - What makes you unique?
    - What resources do you have?

- Weaknesses

  - Where do you need to improve? Do you have customer service problems, high refund rates, cash flow problems, etc.

- Opportunities

  - What outside opportunities do you have? Has your industry recently been mentioned in the press? Have you discovered a new niche or market segment?

- Threats

  - What outside competition do you have? What obstacles do you face?

SWOT analysis can give you a clear picture of where your company is, where it is going and how you can get there. This is a very useful tool for marketing as can discover new ways to position and promote your product.

Planning and Marketing Mix

SECTION 1: TYPES OF PRODUCTS AND PRODUCT TRAITS

The Tangible Products: The physical products or services offered. Example: Lipstick, Televisions, Computers, Typing services, Educational programs, etc.

The Extended Product: Physical products – tangible products – together with a gamut of services going with the products. A computer is a tangible product accompanied with a host of services like software, hardware instructions, canned software programs, maintenance, important parts like hard drive guarantees and peripheral supplies, making it an extended product. Tangible product + accompanying services, guarantees, freebies = Extended Product.

The Generic Products: It relates to the buyer's expectations of basic benefits the product is supposed to shower on the buyer. Example: A computer. The buyer is not interested in the hardware or software or peripherals. He is acquiring a computer for problem solving abilities. A computer therefore is a generic product of problem solving. A nail polish is a generic product of beauty.

The BCG Growth Share Matrix can be used to classify products based on their market growth rate and relative market share. Market growth rate is how quickly the particular market is growing. For example, in technology, there is always something newer and better, meaning high growth and a lot of money to be made. However, as far a grocery stores go, there are always going to be the same basic products, and people will be buying the same basic things. This means there is low growth. Relative market share is how prominent the product is within the market. For example, in terms of stores, stores like Walmart and Target tend to dominate the grocery industry with large market shares, whereas local based stores have a low market share. Based on how the products rate in these two categories, they can be called a dog, problem child, star or cash cow.

A dog is a product with low market growth and low relative market share. It is a product in a slowly growing industry with little recognition. It may break even as far as costs go, but it doesn't have any real potential and ties up a lot of resources for a company. Financially speaking, they are worthless assets.

A problem child, or question mark, is a product with a low relative market share in a fast growing market. Because the market is growing fast, they have a lot of potential to do well, but the low relative market share means that they could fall into the dog category if or when the market slows down. If they gain market share, they could move into the star or cash cow category.

A star is a product with a high market share in a fast growing industry. These are products that lead in their market, and generate a lot of revenue. However, it may require a lot of money to keep the product at the front of their market. When the market slows down there is potential for them to fall to a dog if the product doesn't keep a high market share, but if they do keep a high market share they become cash cows.

A cash cow is a product with a high market share in a slow growing industry. In other words, it is one of the most recognized products in a field that doesn't sustain much change. This is the best type of product to have because it allows the company to make a lot of money, with little investment needed (at this point marketing isn't really necessary). It generates the revenue needed to keep the company functioning, and possibly allow them to expand and turn problem child and star products into cash cows as well.

SECTION 2: THE PRODUCT MIX DECISIONS

Before we proceed to take up product mix decisions, let us see what is PLC – Product Life Cycle.

Product Life Cycle: The systematic study of a product's history will reveal a varying cycle of stages of opportunities and threats, ups and downs that are relevant to any marketing strategy. There are distinct stages in a product's PLC known as Introduction, Growth, Maturity and Decline.

THE STAGES OF PRODUCT LIFE CYCLE

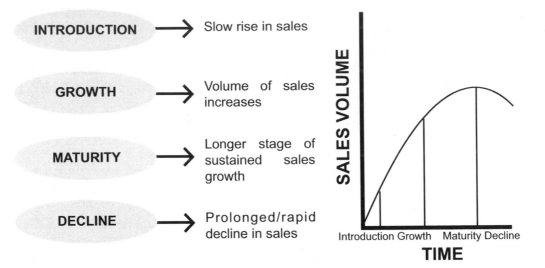

The particular stage at which a product is at the time of preparing the Marketing strategy, has a lot to do with the allocation for each element of the Marketing Mix. The PLC can also be applied to a Product <u>Class</u> (say Perfumes) or to a specific <u>Brand</u> (say Christian Dior or Intimate) or to a product <u>Form</u> (say sprays, roll-ons, etc.). The product policy decisions of a company are taken at three different levels as each company today produces products at a prolific rate.

<u>Product item</u>: A particular version of a product. Example: Sony 'Walkman II'.
<u>Product line</u>: A group of closely related products. Example: All Walkman products of Sony.
<u>Product mix</u>: A number of related products offered. Sony's 'Walkman', HiFi products, etc.

Now let us study the 'width,' 'depth' and 'consistency' of the product mix.

<u>Width</u>: Refers to the number of product lines offered. Mitsubishi produces a range of products from Air conditioners, Machines, Electric Appliances, Cars, etc.

<u>Depth</u>: Refers to the average number of products offered within each product line. LG produces Air conditioning machines with different capacities - 0.5 ton, 1.0 ton, 1.5 tons, 2.0 ton, split AC, etc.

<u>Consistency</u>: How similarly related the offered product lines end use, production and distribution. A product line of Air Conditioners is related in that they all involve electricity. The Product Life Cycle concept has close links with the Adoption and Diffusion processes. The adoption process has a tendency to affect the length of a given product's Life Cycle. Let us now see how a new product is adopted.

The Adoption Process: Unless some buyer buys a product in its introductory stage of PLC, it cannot survive that stage. The adoption processes is a series of stages a potential buyer is likely to go through in order to decide to buy a product and also continue to use the product. There are four stages:

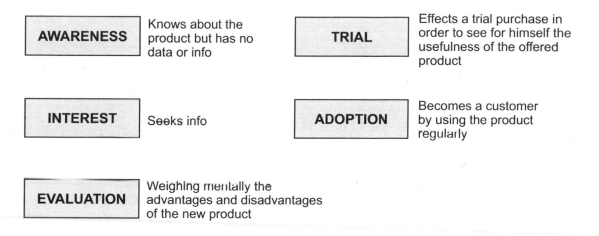

AWARENESS	Knows about the product but has no data or info
TRIAL	Effects a trial purchase in order to see for himself the usefulness of the offered product
INTEREST	Seeks info
ADOPTION	Becomes a customer by using the product regularly
EVALUATION	Weighing mentally the advantages and disadvantages of the new product

The adoption rate depends on:

(1) Relative advantage – product's superiority over others

(2) Compatibility – product's consistency in relation to the buyer's cultural value and lifestyle

(3) Complexity – the relative difficulty in understanding or using the offered product

(4) Divisibility – degree to which the product is allowed for trial use

(5) Communicability – observed product behavior results communicated to others by word of mouth

If the communicability aspect is greater, the chances of the products adoption rate are faster.

The Diffusion Process: How fast a new product spreads throughout a target market is known as the Diffusion process. There are 5 categories of adopters. They are:

1. Innovators,
2. Early adopters
3. Early majority
4. Late majority
5. Laggards

A bell curve will give us a clear picture about the diffusion process:

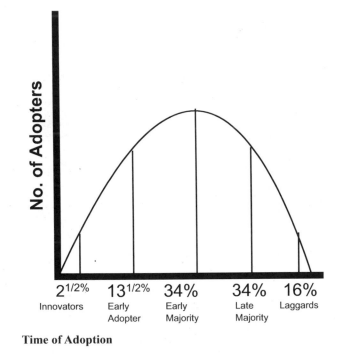

Time of Adoption

From the above you can see that the innovators and early adopters together account for only (2.5 +13.5) = 16%. In other words those who have not yet adopted the product are still a majority – 84%. However, if innovators and early adopters do not adopt, even though they only adopt 16%, the chances of others trying the product are nil and consequently the product is bound to fail in the market.

SECTION 3: CHANNELS OF DISTRIBUTION

The American Marketing Association defines the channel of distribution as "…an organized network of agencies and institutions, which in combination perform all the activities required to link producers with users to accomplish the marketing task…" If any organization really wants to enter a competitive market, its options are: (1) Induce independent channels to promote the organization's products by giving incentives (2) Establish their own franchised outlets.

No product will reach the market unless there is a well thought out distribution system. To do this, it is necessary to bring in the services of intermediates in order to effect a foolproof product distribution system. A channel of distribution is a series of institutions dealing in marketing activities, which facilitates transfers of the goods as well as the title to goods from producer to other intermediates to the ultimate consumer. Let us consider the normal channel employed for both consumer and producer goods.

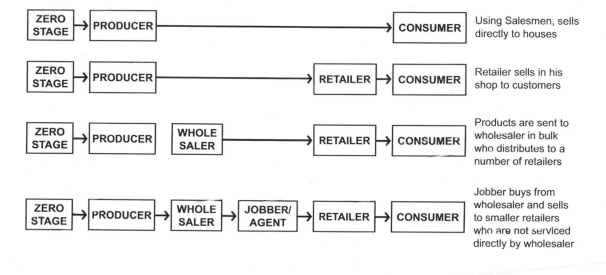

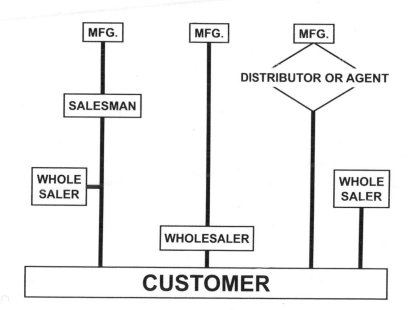

If you want an effective channel, your approach should be to find out what the customer really wants and based on that develop your strategy. Which are the factors that influence channel development?

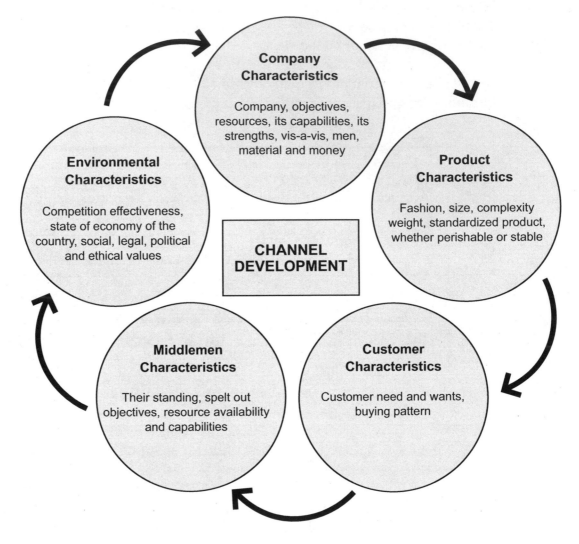

Channel Planning: (1) Should know the type of middlemen required (2) Number of such middlemen in each type (3) Which particular middlemen to use, and (4) How to motivate middlemen.

1. Determining Types of Middlemen:
Dual Distribution: If a unit uses two or more competing channels for its sales of product lines it is known as a Dual Distribution system. Example: Using company outlets and retail outlets.

Facilitating Middlemen: Producer moves goods and title to goods to the ultimate buyer. Transporter moves goods, Bankers finance, Insurers insure the inventory in transit and Marketing Research firms provide information. They are functional middlemen and are known as facilitating middlemen. Channel members use such facilitating middlemen if they are convinced they can carry out all the functions more economically and most efficiently.

2. The number of middlemen to use:
This largely depends on whether you want (a) an intensive (b) selective or (c) exclusive distributor.

(a) Intensive Distribution: Product to be available in as many outlets as possible. Example: Soaps, detergents or cigarettes.

(b) Selective Distribution: Related to distribution in a geographic area restricted to middlemen guided by their perceived performance capability. Industrial products, specialized products and shopping products are distributed on selective distribution basis.

(c) Exclusive Distribution: Having only one exclusive outlet in a geographic area. Some specialty products like Leica Cameras, Rolex watches are distributed on the basis of exclusive distribution.

3. Which particular middlemen to use:
Producers can choose whichever middlemen they like provided the middlemen are willing, capable and ever ready to participate in the channel.

4. How to motivate middlemen:
Trade promotions, selective promotional allowances to take care of advertising costs, publicity, and good use of product displays – all these are some of the motivational tools used by producers to make middlemen work better. Additionally, a salesman's rapport with the middlemen goes a long way in motivating middlemen.

Personal Selling
In the realm of personal selling (selling things in person) two of the main theories are missionary selling and relationship selling. Missionary selling involves seeking out new customers and convincing them to buy the product for the first time. This would be done, for example, by door to door salespeople. The idea is to convince the buyer to have faith in the product (which is where the name came from). Generally this approach is considered to consume more time, energy and resources than its alternate, relationship selling. Relationship selling follows the theory that it is easier to maintain a client than to find a new one. The idea is to start a genuine relationship with the client, to listen to their needs and concerns, so that they will keep coming back.

SECTION 4: PRODUCT PROMOTION EFFORTS

Promotion is a company's attempt to generate sales through effective communication to any group of buyers. The forms of promotion are: advertising, personal selling, sales promotion and publicity.

Now let us suppose you have an excellent product with all the attributes needed, with a price tag that is attractive, and with a system that makes the product easily available to the consumer. You have advantages of product, price and distribution. Will this situation generate excellent sales? The answer is a definite no! If a company wants to generate exceptional sales, it must spend time in creating a meaningful and effective program of communication and promotion. Communication is a process of influencing other's behavior pattern. So, it is communication – meaningful and effective communication - that is the basic building block of any promotional activity. A communication model consists of:

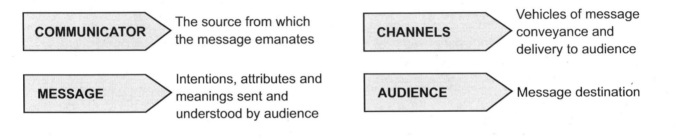

COMMUNICATOR — The source from which the message emanates

MESSAGE — Intentions, attributes and meanings sent and understood by audience

CHANNELS — Vehicles of message conveyance and delivery to audience

AUDIENCE — Message destination

To make a purchase a buyer has to be influenced and an effective communication does just that. There are channels of influence and let us see them now:

CHANNELS OF INFLUENCE

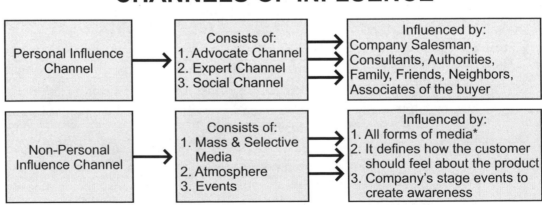

Personal Influence Channel → Consists of:
1. Advocate Channel
2. Expert Channel
3. Social Channel
→ Influenced by: Company Salesman, Consultants, Authorities, Family, Friends, Neighbors, Associates of the buyer

Non-Personal Influence Channel → Consists of:
1. Mass & Selective Media
2. Atmosphere
3. Events
→ Influenced by:
1. All forms of media*
2. It defines how the customer should feel about the product
3. Company's stage events to create awareness

* (A) Print media like newspapers, magazines; Broadcast media like radio, television; Information technology media like websites, emails, etc. (B) Outdoor media like billboards, etc.

Message: Meaningful and effective communication needs (1) to identify the target audience, and (2) which channels to use in order to reach the target audience. The designing of the message should be in keeping with the target audience and selected channels. According to John C. Maloney "…is advertising believability really important…" "… No single advertisement is likely to produce absolute 'belief' in a product. Rather each advertisement is likely to make its most significant contribution by nudging the consumer onto and along the path of the adoption process…"

Vertical channels occur when all the levels of production and distribution for a product are owned by the same person. For example, it would be a vertical channel if a person owns the factory their product is made in, a trucking store to ship it around the country and retail stores to sell the product in. This creates a channel through which the product is produced.

Horizontal channels are all essentially on the same level of production. For example, a Walmart store often has a McDonald's store in them. Both are on the same level because they sell directly to a consumer, and, although they are entirely different stores, they both benefit from teaming up together. For example, horizontal channels also occur when a number of factories merge.

THE PROMOTION MIX

A promotion mix consists of (1) Personal Selling (2) Advertising (3) Sales Promotion, and (4) Public Relations. Some have included packaging also in the promotion mix but considering it as an essential extension and attribute of a product, it can safely be taken as an extended product form rather than part of a product mix.

PROMOTION MIX IN A NUTSHELL

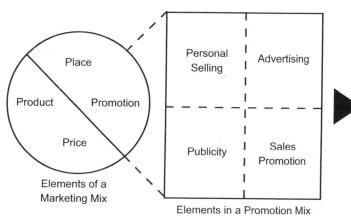

To be effective, there should be a perfect blend of all the elements of a Promotion Mix. This ensures achieving organizational objectives – stimulated sales and better bottomlines.

Personal Selling: Ensures face to face contact between company's salesman and the buyer. A good salesman who enjoys good personal rapport with a buyer can achieve exceptional results.

Advertising: Helps to identify the needed products

Sales promotion: Programs designed to directly or indirectly stimulate sales

Sales: Sales contests, consumer contests, discount sales, etc.

Publicity: Publicity is to maintain good will as well as to create a favorable impression about the company and its products.

Brief Objectives of Promotions:

1. To create awareness
2. To provide information about the company and its products
3. To explain company programs
4. To induce a buyer for a product trial
5. Coaxing middlemen to stock products
6. To create customer loyalty
7. Try to reduce seasonal fluctuation by offering special programs during off season

There are two different ways to promote a product: push strategy and pull strategy. To push a product involves bringing the product to the customer, and making sure they are aware of it. The developers market it to the manufacturers who market it to the stores who market it to the buyers. They may put up window displays or offer special deals, anything to get the buyer to become aware of the product. Pull strategy involves bring the customer to the product. This strategy involves creating a demand for the product that will pull it through the stages. For example, if there is a TV commercial advertising the product, people will request it in the stores. The stores will then seek the product from manufacturers and so on.

SECTION 5: ADVERTISING

Methods of marketing include direct and indirect marketing. Direct marketing involves a hands on approach. Internet ads, newspaper ads, TV commercials, telemarketers and coupons are all types of direct advertising. Anything which is done by the company to directly generating demand and interest in their products is considered direct advertising. Indirect advertising, on the other hand, is harder to pin down. This is when advertising occurs, but in a less forceful way. For example, word of mouth advertising is when a person recommends a product they like. Also, if a company donates money to a cause and their name is listed it is also a form of indirect advertising.

Advocacy advertising is advertising which is designed to support one side of a controversial issue. Essentially, it is advertising a person's viewpoint and they are trying to persuade others of their position. An example would be if a person puts a large sign in their yard advocating a political candidate. Or, if a person writes an article advocating gun control.

SECTION 6: PRICE DETERMINATION

Macroeconomic theory as well as general equilibrium theory emphasizes the predominance of price theory in economics for over a century now. However, in today's business, so many variables such as household consumption increase in the disposable income pattern of people, agricultural, industrial, electronics and knowledge revolutions all put their stamps on the pricing mechanism of companies all over the world. The non-pricing variables are to be studied and dealt with in your overall price determination.

Where do pricing decisions assume significance?

(1) If a unit sets a price for the first time when a new product is introduced, there is always an uncertainty on the pricing front. Likewise, if a unit introduces a product into a new and untried market segment, it has a problem at hand. (2) When a unit has to consider initiating a price revision, it has to face uncertainties. The price change may be on account of sudden demand fluctuations or increased costs. (3) Again if a competitor initiates a revision in price, the unit has no choice except to toe the line or face erosion in sales. (4) If a unit produces many products interrelated by costs or demands, the pricing decision becomes a real problem. How to determine an optimal price relationship for the individual products in the product line? It is definitely a mind-boggling problem.

PRICE ELASTICITY

A price elasticity of -1 tells us that sales will rise/fall by an identical percentage change as price falls/rises. Likewise, a price elasticity of which is greater than -1 indicates that sales will rise/fall by such percentage point that is more than the price fall/rise. And finally, a price elasticity of less than -1 tell us that sales will rise/fall by less than price falls/rises in terms of percentage. In the first case there won't be any change in the total revenue. In the second case the total revenue is likely to rise. And in the third case, there is bound to be a total revenue fall. This is a most important factor every company has to bear in mind before attempting any revision in product price.

What are the objectives in price fixing?

1. **Market Penetration Objective:** They start with relatively low price, in order to obtain a bigger market share. Any market which is price sensitive can offer a better sales volume with a small cut in price. Also, they resort to this objective if they are facing potential competition whose efforts the company has to nullify.

2. **Market Skimming Objective:** In any market, there are buyers who are willing to pay a higher price if they perceive the value of the product is more compared to other products. Also, if they find that a higher price tag has no imminent danger of coaxing competition to enter in a big way.

3. **Early Recovery Objective:** The pricing is done in such a way that the company is assured of rapid recovery of cash.

4. **Satisfying Objective:** A satisfactory rate of return is aimed through this pricing objective.

5. **Product line promotion Objective:** It is possible that setting a price for a product even at a small loss increases the volume of sales of the complete product line. They refer to this pricing objective as "loss-leader" pricing.

One way of characterizing the demand for goods is as either elastic or inelastic. When the demand for a good is elastic, this means it is determined on price. For example, the demand for candy tends to be elastic because people only want to buy it if it is inexpensive, and the demand for it goes down if it becomes expensive. Inelastic products are products that people will buy no matter what the cost. Gas is one such product. Although people complain about rising prices, they still buy it because they need it.

PRICING MODELS

1. **Cost oriented pricing:** It is normally covering all costs, which includes an arbitrary allocation of overhead as a percentage of operating costs.

2. **Mark-up pricing:** the important mark-up pricing is cost-plus pricing in which a certain fixed percentage is added to the product cost. It is common in retail business.

3. **Target pricing:** It is a pricing practice in which price is determined on the basis of a specified target rate of return on the total costs arrived at on the basis of an estimated standard volume.

4. **Demand oriented pricing:** It is a simple economic pricing where a higher price is charged when there is a heavy demand and a reduced price charged when the demand slips.

5. **Price discrimination:** A particular product is marketed at two or more prices either on the basis of customer, or on the basis of product version (products vary with slight variations) or, on the basis of place (theater seats are place-based price discrimination).

6. **Competition oriented pricing:** The company waits for competitors to make the first move and then follows in the price revision.

7. **Going rate pricing (Imitative pricing):** It is a type of competition oriented pricing where a unit holds its price at an average level charged by the industry.

8. **Sealed bid pricing:** It is also a type of competition oriented pricing where companies compete on the basis of bids. Example: original equipment manufacturers, defense contracts, public work contracts, etc.

MARKUP

Markup is the difference between the actual price of the product to the store and the price they sell the product for. In other words, markup is the difference between wholesale price and retail price. Markup can be determined as either a percentage or an actual value. For example, if the wholesale price of a product is $10 and it is sold by the store for $20, the markup is $10 or 100%. It is 100% because the price doubled, or the $10 added is the total wholesale price. Also, if the wholesale price of an item was $100 and the markup percentage was 25%, the retail price would be $125.

BREAK EVEN POINT

The break even point is where the cost of producing a product equals the profit made from selling it. For example, it might cost a company $30,000 dollars to produce 5,000 couches. If they only sell 4,000 couches, they will have lost a lot of money. If they sell 6,000 couches they will make a lot of money. However, if they sell 5,000 couches they will break even. They won't have lost any money, but they won't have made any money. To calculate the break even point you must determine total costs, which includes fixed costs and variable costs, and total revenue.

Fixed costs are costs which are incurred once and don't change. For example, a factory buys a new machine. They only pay for that machine once. On the other hand, variable costs are the cost that is incurred with each new unit of product produced. For example, a taffy factory buys their machine (the fixed cost) but for each sheet of taffy they produce they have to buy ingredients.

For example, a toy factory, just going into business, buys two machines at $3,000 each. For each toy they produce, they must pay 75 cents. However, they sell the toys for five dollars. Assume that there are no other costs to the business, and that the business will sell all the products it makes. To determine how many toys they must sell to break even, the formula would be: (Variable Costs * Volume) + Total Costs = (Price * Volume) The total cost would be $6,000 + 0.75x. The total revenue would be $5x (x will represent the number of toys produced and the number sold because we want them to be equal). Therefore, the equation is:

$6,000 + $0.75x = $5x
$6,000 = $5x − $0.75x
x = $6,000/ ($5-$0.75)
x= 1,411.8

The business must sell at least 1,412 toys to break even.

SECTION 6: MARKETING EFFORT CONTROL

Any effort needs control. Without control you do not know whether your efforts are bearing fruit as desired. Without control you know not whether you are on the track or off the track or heading in the right direction or in the opposite.

A marketing control sub-system aims to control the efficiency of its sales team, the efficiency of its advertising effectiveness, the efficiency of its distribution channel effectiveness, the efficiency of its product transportation effectiveness, the effectiveness of its annual plans and monthly targets. Let us now see the 4 elements of a control system:

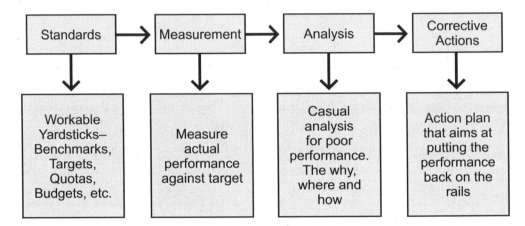

The most important control measures are aimed at expense and revenue deviation analysis of which the ratio analysis is essential. Some of the ratio analysis that gives you a fair picture of the "goings on" thereby presenting you with a platform for corrective action are: (1) Expense to sales ratios (Cost per sales call, cost incurred to prospect, advertisement expenses to sales, etc). (2) Sales to gross profit ratios. (3) Percentage of returned goods. (4) Current sales to order backlog ratios. (5) Individual salesman turnover. (6) Number of months inventory held in factory and in distributor's warehouse. (7) Bad debts ratio. (8) ABC analysis of sales concentration (i.e., sales percentage of top 20 percent customers), etc. A standard control chart model can be gainfully employed to control expenses.

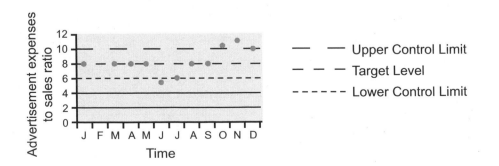

From the above chart you can see that the ratio of expenses to sales is within the targeted level most of the target period, but during the final stages of the target period it goes beyond the upper control limit, which is likely to happen as towards the end there will be a spurt in activity to reach overall targets.

Writing a Marketing Plan

Writing and creating a marketing plan takes you through every step of the process of taking a new product to market, if done correctly. Now we'll take some of the information we've already learned about and put it into practice, while learning some new things along the way.

AOSTC is a tool for creating marketing plans:

Analysis
Objectives
Strategies
Tactics
Controls

The first step, analysis includes the SWOT test as well as other important factors like political climate, trends, laws and regulations, etc.

The seconds step, objectives is where you need to create objectives using the SMART test. **SMART** stands for:

Specific
Measurable
Achievable
Realistic
Timed

The third step is creating a strategy. What is the target market that you are going after? What is the demographic? What makes this segment the best?

The fourth step is tactics. This is where the Four P's come into play again.

Price
Place
Product
Promotion

Determine the specifics of each category.

Price – Will the product be at, above or below the competition?
Place – How will the product be sold or distributed?
Product – Are there any special features? Will it be bundled?
Promotion – How will it be marketed? Online? Through retailers? Direct mail?

The fifth step is controls. These refer to the hard aspects of running any business or campaign such as market date, start up costs, production costs, commissions, etc.

Legal Aspects of Marketing

LEGISLATION

The Sherman Antitrust Act was passed in 1890 and was the first act to work against monopolies (or trusts) and cartels. It made it illegal for any contract, deal, conspiracy or scheme to restrain trade, and allowed the government the right to investigate and take legal action against any company that did. This would therefore include when large companies formed cartels to drive up prices, or when one company grew large enough to put all others out of business. The law wasn't really recognized until the presidency of Theodore Roosevelt who became known as a "trustbuster" for using it to bring down major monopolies.

The Clayton Act (or Clayton Antitrust Act) was passed in 1914 as an amendment to the Sherman Antitrust Act to clarify the prohibited actions. For example, it specifically mentioned local price cuts (lowering the price in only one area to put competition out of business and then raising prices) and exclusive sales contracts. It also legalized strikes and boycotts.

The Robinson-Patman Act was passed in 1936 and amended the Clayton Act. The act had specifically mentioned local price cuts, but the Robinson-Patman Act extended it to include other forms of price discrimination. The main focus was on price discrimination from wholesalers to retailers. Chain stores, because of their size, were often able to get the same products for cheaper and were able to profitably undersell their competition. The act made it illegal for wholesalers to sell a product for less to one store than another. Because of this it is often referred to as the "chain store act."

The Federal Trade Commission Act was passed in 1914. It prevents companies from using unfair or deceptive business practices, and gives the government the right to issue cease and desist orders. It created the Federal Trade Commission (FTC), a five person board created to regulate unfair business practices. Members of the FTC are appointed for overlapping seven year terms and no more than three members can be from the same party.

TAXES

Tariffs are taxes levied on goods imported from (or exported to) another country. Typically this is done for two reasons: to make locally made goods more attractive and to increase government revenue. The reason that tariffs make locally made goods more attractive is because it means that the foreign products have the added expense, and it helps allow the locally made good to be priced lower. However, sometimes it can still be cheaper to buy those products even with the added tax.

The North American Free Trade Agreement (NAFTA) established one of the largest free trade zones in the world. It eliminated almost all tariffs between trade through Canada, the United States and Mexico.

Sample Test Questions

1) Which of the following is NOT one of the Four P's?

    A) Price
    B) Promotion
    C) Production
    D) Place
    E) None of the above

The correct answer is C:) Production. The Four P's are (1) Product (2) Place (3) Promotion and (4) Price.

2) Which of the following BEST describes pull strategy promotion?

    A) Bringing the product to the consumer.
    B) Bringing the consumer to the product.
    C) Creating a demand for the product so that the consumer will seek it through their local stores.
    D) Pulling the product to the front of the store so consumers are more likely to be aware of it.
    E) Both B and C

The correct answer is E:) Both B and C. Pull strategy involves creating a demand for the product that will pull it through the stages, such as with a TV commercial. Answers A and D describe push strategy promotion.

3) _____ refers to a company's employment of inputs, such as men, material and money, into the company's overall marketing process in order to generate sales.

    A) Marketing mix
    B) Marketing allocation
    C) Marketing response
    D) Marketing effort
    E) None of the above

The correct answer is D:) Marketing effort.

4)   Which of the following BEST describes the meaning of elastic in marketing?

   A) A product which holds its shape well.
   B) A product which people will buy no matter what price it is.
   C) A product which people will not buy if it is too expensive.
   D) A product which starts out selling good, but the demand for it does not last.
   E) A product which does sell well at first, but demand for it grows.

The correct answer is C:) A product which people will not buy if it is too expensive. On the other hand, inelastic products are products which people will buy no matter what price they are.

5) _____ refers to a company's overall objectives, tactics, policies and guide-lines that govern over a period of that company's marketing effort.

   A) Marketing mix
   B) Marketing allocation
   C) Marketing response
   D) Marketing strategy
   E) None of the above

The correct answer is D:) Marketing strategy.

6)   Which of the following describes cognitive dissonance?

   A) Advertising which is designed to support one side of a controversial issue.
   B) Starting a genuine relationship with the client and listening to their needs and concerns.
   C) Seeking out new customers and convincing them to buy the product for the first time.
   D) When a person has second thoughts about whether they purchased the correct product.
   E) None of the above

The correct answer is D:) When a person has second thoughts about whether they purchased the correct product. This can occur because they later realize they didn't really want or need it, or because they see advertisements for a competitive product.

7) _____ is the most important task of the Marketing Department to find out the optimum setting for its Marketing Decision Variables.

    A) Marketing mix
    B) Marketing allocation
    C) Marketing response
    D) Marketing effort
    E) None of the above

The correct answer is A:) Marketing mix.

8) Which of the following describes a star product?

    A) High market growth and high relative market share
    B) High market growth and low relative market share
    C) Low market growth and high relative market share
    D) Low market growth and low relative market share
    E) None of the above

The correct answer is A:) High market growth and high relative market share. These are products that lead in their fast growing market, and generate a lot of revenue.

9) _____ is related to the pattern of sales to the marketing effort.

    A) Marketing mix
    B) Marketing allocation
    C) Marketing response
    D) Marketing strategy
    E) None of the above

The correct answer is C:) Marketing response.

10) If a product has a retail price $550, and the markup is 10%, what was the whole-sale price?

    A) $50
    B) $450
    C) $500
    D) $540
    E) Cannot be determined without more information

The correct answer is C:) $500. 10% of $500 is $50. $500+$50= $550.

11) Which is the following is NOT a market segmentation variable?

    A) Population
    B) Benefits sought
    C) Spending pattern
    D) Marketing
    E) None of the above

The correct answer is D:) Marketing. Market segmentation variables can include all demographics, age, race, occupation as well as things such as personality and lifestyle.

12) If a product has a wholesale price of $30 and a markup of 200%, what is its retail price?

    A) $32
    B) $50
    C) $90
    D) $200
    E) $230

The correct answer is C:) $90. 30+200% = 30+30(2.00) = 30+60 – 90.

13) Kbrand corporation wants to markup their alarm clocks 30% above their cost of $15. What would be the cost to the consumer?

    A) $19.50
    B) $10
    C) $20
    D) $22.50
    E) None of the above

The correct answer is A:) $19.50.

14) Marketing based on brand loyalty would be considered what type of segmentation?

    A) Demographic
    B) Geographic
    C) Psychographic
    D) Behavioral
    E) None of the above

The correct answer is D:) Behavioral. Behavioral segmentation is based on people's attitude toward the product.

15) Which of the following does the S stand for in SWOT analysis?

    A) Strategy
    B) Strength
    C) Superior
    D) Status
    E) None of the above

The correct answer is B:) Strength.

16) A new law regulating the amount of toxic fumes a factory is allowed to produce would be considered what type of change?

    A) Social
    B) Economic
    C) Technological
    D) Political
    E) Legal

The correct answer is E:) Legal. Legal changes can affect how businesses are allowed to market and function.

17) Which of the following is the correct path of a product lifecycle?

    A) Introduction, growth, reinvention, decline
    B) Market demand, production, growth, decline
    C) Market demand, production, decline, reinvention
    D) Introduction, growth, maturity, decline
    E) None of the above

The correct answer is D:) Introduction, growth, maturity, decline. Although many companies at the decline period add new features or reinvent the product to gain more sales, this is considered a "re-start" of the product lifecycle.

18) A war in the Middle East causes gas prices to rise. This is what type of change?

    A) Social
    B) Economic
    C) Technological
    D) Political
    E) Legal

The correct answer is D:) Political. Political changes can affect international trade, and in this case that caused gas prices to rise.

19) Which of the following refers to the number of product lines offered?

    A) Width
    B) Depth
    C) Consistency
    D) Line
    E) None of the above

The correct answer is A:) Width. Width to the number of product lines offered. For example, Mitsubishi produces a range of products from air conditioners, machines, electric appliances, cars, etc.

20) Which of the following was the first act to work against monopolies?

    A) Sherman Antitrust Act
    B) Clayton Act
    C) Robinson-Patman Act
    D) Federal Trade Commission Act
    E) North American Free Trade Agreement

The correct answer is A:) Sherman Antitrust Act. The Sherman Antitrust Act was passed in 1890 and was the first act to work against monopolies (or trusts) and cartels.

21) Which of the following refers to how similarly related the offered product lines in end use, production and distribution?

    A) Width
    B) Depth
    C) Consistency
    D) Line
    E) None of the above

The correct answer is C:) Consistency.

22) Which act is also known as the "Chain Store Act"?

    A) Sherman Antitrust Act
    B) Clayton Act
    C) Robinson-Patman Act
    D) Federal Trade Commission Act
    E) North American Free Trade Agreement

The correct answer is C:) Robinson-Patman Act. The act made price discrimination between wholesalers and retailers illegal.

23) Which of the following refers to the average number of products offered within each product line?

    A) Width
    B) Depth
    C) Consistency
    D) Line
    E) None of the above

The correct answer is B:) Depth. This refers to the average number of products offered within each product line. For example, LG produces Air conditioning machines with different capacities - 0.5 ton, 1.0 ton, 1.5 tons, 2.0 ton, split AC, etc.

24) A company buys 10 new machines to make baseball hats and each costs $1,200. They must pay 20 cents for each hat they make. They sell their hats for $5 each. They only plan to make as many as they need to break even. How many must they make (assuming they sell all the hats they make)?

    A) 1500
    B) 2000
    C) 2500
    D) 3000
    E) 3500

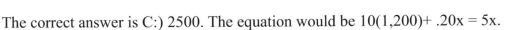

The correct answer is C:) 2500. The equation would be 10(1,200)+ .20x = 5x.

25) A grouping of consumers with similar needs and wants is called

    A) Market segmentation
    B) Product quality
    C) Product differentiation
    D) Product diversification
    E) Market expansion

The correct answer is A:) Market segmentation. Any subset or a number of such subsets may be taken in as a target audience in that market and approached with a specific marketing mix. This is called market segmentation.

26) Which of the following is a heterogeneous product?

    A) Cars
    B) Bubble wrap
    C) Produce
    D) Nails
    E) None of the above

The correct answer is C:) Produce.

27) When existing products are marketed to new groups it is called

    A) Market segmentation
    B) Product quality
    C) Product differentiation
    D) Product diversification
    E) Market expansion

The correct answer is E:) Market expansion.

28) Which of the following best describes advocacy advertising?

    A) Advertising which is designed to support one side of a controversial issue.
    B) Starting a genuine relationship with the client and listening to their needs and concerns.
    C) Seeking out new customers and convincing them to buy the product for the first time.
    D) When a person has second thoughts about whether they purchased the correct product.
    E) None of the above

The correct answer is A:) Advertising which is designed to support one side of a controversial issue. Essentially, it is advertising a person's viewpoint and they are trying to persuade others of their position.

29) This area is reviewed before introduction of a product into market and is completed by the engineering department.

   A) Market segmentation
   B) Product quality
   C) Product differentiation
   D) Product diversification
   E) Market expansion

The correct answer is B:) Product quality. Product quality should be reviewed and completed well before a product hits the market.

30) What a marketing department does to show the benefits of a new product compared to other existing products.

   A) Market segmentation
   B) Product quality
   C) Product differentiation
   D) Product diversification
   E) Market expansion

The correct answer is C:) Product differentiation.

31) A salesperson that closely manages the relationship between physician and pharmaceutical companies including placing orders, providing samples and visiting the physician is called what?

   A) Service salesperson
   B) Multi-level-marketing salesperson
   C) Missionary salesperson
   D) Direct salesperson
   E) None of the above

The correct answer is C:) Missionary salesperson. Although the name is somewhat of a misnomer, a missionary salesperson closely manages the relationship between manufacturer and their customers.

32) This is done to increase product lines, avoiding seasonal fluctuations in demand and achieving a higher growth rate.

 A) Market segmentation
 B) Product quality
 C) Product differentiation
 D) Product diversification
 E) Market expansion

The correct answer is E:) Market expansion. Market expansion can increase product lines, insulate a company from relying financially on one product, avoid seasonal fluctuations by adding more products to the marketing mix and help achieve a higher growth rate.

33) Which of the following is most likely an inelastic product?

 A) Chocolate
 B) A new camera
 C) Going out to dinner
 D) Medicine
 E) All of the above are elastic

The correct answer is D:) Medicine. Whether or not it is expensive, people are likely to buy the medicine that they need. On the other hand chocolate, a new camera and going out to dinner are all luxury activities that people generally do only if it is convenient and they can afford to do it.

34) An aftermarket car parts manufacturer sells their product to a distributor who then sells directly to retail car accessory stores. The manufacturer sells their product for $50 to the distributor who marks up the product 25% before selling to the retailer. The retailer then has a 100% markup on the product sold to the ultimate consumer. What is the price a retail customer will pay?

 A) $125
 B) $150
 C) $175
 D) $200
 E) $225

The correct answer is A:) $125. The initial price is $50. The markup the distributor adds is $12.50, making the product cost $62.50 to the retailer. Their markup is 100% of the product cost, or $62.50. $62.50 for the product plus $62.50 for the markup makes this item $125 for the ultimate consumer.

35) Which of the following best describes tariffs?

    A) Taxes on goods imported from or exported to another country.
    B) Any tax which is instituted by a national government.
    C) A tax which applies only to products made in a certain country.
    D) A percentage of any sold product which must be paid to the government.
    E) Both A and C

The correct answer is A:) Taxes on goods imported from or exported to another country.

36) Sending a customer a postcard in the mail detailing a website with special pricing is a form of

    A) Public relations
    B) Direct marketing
    C) Multi-level-marketing
    D) Differentiated marketing
    E) Customized marketing

The correct answer is B:) Direct marketing. If this marketing program had been only to a select demographic or target audience, it may have been considered customized marketing. However, since it was not, it falls under the category of direct marketing.

37) Which of the following describes a problem child product?

    A) High market growth and high relative market share
    B) High market growth and low relative market share
    C) Low market growth and high relative market share
    D) Low market growth and low relative market share
    E) None of the above

The correct answer is B:) High market growth and low relative market share. They are called problem children because the market is growing fast and they have a lot of potential to do well, but the low relative market share means that they could fall into the dog category if or when the market slows down.

38) Clothing is considered

  A) Hard goods
  B) Electronics
  C) Soft goods
  D) Non-durable goods
  E) None of the above

The correct answer is C:) Soft goods. Textiles of any kind are referred to as soft goods.

39) Which type of product does a company NOT want to have?

  A) Cash cow
  B) Star
  C) Dog
  D) Problem child
  E) Question mark

The correct answer is C:) Dog. It may break even as far as costs go, but it doesn't have any real potential and ties up a lot of resources for a company. Financially speaking they are worthless assets.

40) Janipo Corporation owns three different apparel companies. One company is targeted to infants, one to plus size women and one to tweens. This is an example of

  A) Public relations
  B) Direct marketing
  C) Multi-level-marketing
  D) Differentiated marketing
  E) Customized marketing

The correct answer is D:) Differentiated marketing. In differentiated marketing, sub-groups such as (1) Men (2) Women (3) Children (4) Youth, and (5) Elderly are created and the company offers differentiated products to suit the individual consumer of each such sub group.

41) Which of the following is an example of direct advertising?

    A) Internet ads
    B) Newspaper ads
    C) TV commercial
    D) Telemarketing
    E) All of the above

The correct answer is E:) All of the above. All of the methods listed are direct attempts by the company to promote their product.

42) An air conditioner is a type of

    A) Hard goods
    B) Electronics
    C) Soft goods
    D) Durable goods
    E) None of the above

The correct answer is D:) Durable goods. These tangible goods (actual goods), once bought, will satisfy for many years and include items such as air conditioners, appliances, etc.

43) If the economy falls into a sudden recession it would be considered what type of change?

    A) Social
    B) Economic
    C) Technological
    D) Political
    E) Legal

The correct answer is B:) Economic. Changes in inflation, interest rates and average wages are also economic changes.

44) Once the first level of Maslow's Hierarchy of Needs is met, consumers would be focused on which of the following?

A) Housing in a safe area
B) Groceries
C) Products related to self-esteem
D) Church tithes
E) Charity

The correct answer is C:) Products related to self-esteem. The first level deals with the primary needs of a person such as food, water, shelter, etc. Once that need is met, the second level is presented which deals with self-esteem.

45) A person has a disposable income of $700 and a discretionary income of $300. What are their cost of living expenses?

A) $300
B) $400
C) $500
D) $700
E) $1,000

The correct answer is B:) $400. Discretionary income is the leftover income after cost of living. Therefore cost of living must be $700-$300 or $400.

46) Christy's Blinds wants to advertise in the local direct mail magazine. The cost is $1400 for 10,000 homes. Instead of paying the direct mail magazine in cash, the company trades blinds for the advertising space. This is called

A) Public relations
B) Importing
C) Good business practice
D) Barter
E) Exporting

The correct answer is D:) Barter. Exchanging product, service or merchandise for anything other than cash is called bartering.

47) Which of the following was specifically mentioned in the Clayton Act?

    A) Conspiracies
    B) Schemes
    C) Strikes
    D) Boycotts
    E) Both C and D

The correct answer is E:) Both C and D. Strikes and boycotts were both legalized through the Clayton Act. However, conspiracies and schemes were mentioned in the Sherman Antitrust Act, not the Clayton Act.

48) This step in the sales process identifies potential customers

    A) Presenting
    B) Researching
    C) Prospecting
    D) Segmenting
    E) None of the above

The correct answer is C:) Prospecting.

49) If a business buys a new machine for 4,000 and each unit they produce costs them 5 cents, what must they charge for each unit to break even if they make and sell 500 units? Choose closest answer.

    A) $2
    B) $5
    C) $9
    D) $12
    E) $20

The correct answer is C:) $9. The equation would be 4,000+.05(500) = x (500), where x is the price.

50) A commission paid to a sales person, sometimes referred to as a "spiff" is also called what?

    A) Hush money
    B) Collateral
    C) Advances
    D) Push money
    E) None of the above

The correct answer is D:) Push money.

51) Which of the following is most likely a consumer product?

    A) Computer
    B) Iron
    C) Machines
    D) Steel
    E) All of the above are industrial goods

The correct answer is A:) Computer. Of the products listed, computers are the most likely to be bought for private use.

52) What is the average response rate for direct mail marketing?

    A) 2.6%
    B) 2%
    C) 10%
    D) 8%
    E) 4.1%

The correct answer is A:) 2.6%. Typically, a response rate of 2-3% is considered a successful campaign. However, those numbers can fluctuate on the industry and when considering justification, the cost of the mailing should be a consideration.

53) Which of the following eliminated tariffs between trade through Canada, the United States and Mexico?

    A) Sherman Antitrust Act
    B) Clayton Act
    C) Robinson-Patman Act
    D) Federal Trade Commission Act
    E) North American Free Trade Agreement

The correct answer is E:) North American Free Trade Agreement.

54) Producing a product for use in another country is called

    A) Exporting
    B) Wholesaling
    C) Franchising
    D) Licensing
    E) Importing

The correct answer is A:) Exporting.

55) Which of the following would NOT be considered a tariff?

    A) A government tax on oil imported from Saudi Arabia to the United States.
    B) A tax on toys being outsourced to China, and then shipped back to the United States.
    C) A sales tax on oranges grown in California and shipped to stores in Maine.
    D) A tax on German chocolate imported to the United States.
    E) All of the above are considered tariffs.

The correct answer is C:) A sales tax on oranges grown in California and shipped to stores in Maine. Tariffs apply when products are imported from or exported to another country. California and Maine are both in the United States.

56) Disney Corporation gives ABC corporation permission to put Mickey Mouse on their lunch boxes for a fee. What is this called?

   A) Exporting
   B) Wholesaling
   C) Franchising
   D) Licensing
   E) Importing

The correct answer is D:) Licensing.

57) Which type of product does a company most want to have?

   A) Cash cow
   B) Star
   C) Dog
   D) Problem child
   E) Question mark

The correct answer is A:) Cash cow. This is the best type of product to have because it allows the company to make a lot of money, with little investment needed.

58) John has an amazing restaurant. It is successfully, busy and unique. John decides that other people may want to open a restaurant just like his. By giving permission to copy the concept, help with recipes and consulting advice, Mary agrees to pay an up-front fee and a portion of her profits to John. What is this called?

   A) Exporting
   B) Wholesaling
   C) Franchising
   D) Licensing
   E) Importing

The correct answer is C:) Franchising. The franchisee may also be required to sign a list of rules or other operating agreements to follow in addition to providing a royalty on all sales to the franchisor. Examples of franchises are McDonald's, Subway, and UPS store locations.

59) Segmentation based on what part of the country a person lives in would be classified as

    A) Demographic
    B) Geographic
    C) Psychographic
    D) Behavioral
    E) None of the above

The correct answer is B:) Geographic. Geographic segmentation is segmentation based on location.

60) The process of bringing in goods from a foreign country for the purpose of selling them is called what?

    A) Exporting
    B) Wholesaling
    C) Franchising
    D) Licensing
    E) Importing

The correct answer is E:) Importing.

61) In 1794, the invention of the cotton gin changed the South by making it far more profitable to mass produce cotton. This change is considered to have been

    A) Social
    B) Economic
    C) Technological
    D) Political
    E) Legal

The correct answer is C:) Technological. Technology affects all levels of marketing. This makes keeping up with the changes an important element of marketing.

62) Purchasing from the manufacturer and reselling to the retailer is called what?

A) Exporting
B) Wholesaling
C) Franchising
D) Licensing
E) Importing

The correct answer is B:) Wholesaling.

63) Which of the following was passed as an amendment to the Sherman Antitrust Act to clarify it?

A) Sherman Antitrust Act
B) Clayton Act
C) Robinson-Patman Act
D) Federal Trade Commission Act
E) North American Free Trade Agreement

The correct answer is B:) Clayton Act.

64) Which of the following would NOT be a SMART objective?

A) To reduce costs in production 5% by January 2015
B) To increase sales by 10% in Q3
C) To hire three researchers by the end of next month
D) To open two new locations
E) To gain 15% of the market share by March 2010

The correct answer is D:) To open two new locations. This item is not specific enough, nor timed so it would NOT be considered a SMART objective.

65) A paper company has been selling paper to an office building for over 20 years. Their selling style would be best classified as

A) Relationship
B) Technological
C) Demographical
D) Missionary
E) None of the above

The correct answer is A:) Relationship. Relationship selling follows the theory that it is easier to maintain a client than to find a new one.

66) The O in SWOT analysis stands for what?

   A) Online
   B) Organization
   C) Ornamentation
   D) Opportunities
   E) None of the above

The correct answer is D:) Opportunities.

67) Which of the following is a homogeneous product?

   A) Produce
   B) Donuts
   C) Nails
   D) Custom clothing
   E) None of the above

The correct answer is C:) Nails.

68) When you can only buy the latest video game from Walmart, the manufacturer for that game is participating in

   A) Incentive distribution
   B) Geographic distribution
   C) Exclusive distribution
   D) Determined distribution
   E) None of the above

The correct answer is C:) Exclusive distribution. Exclusive distribution is when a company determines one retailer per country, state or city will be the only way of purchasing their product.

69) Which of the following products is most likely elastic?

   A) Medicine
   B) Candy
   C) Gas
   D) Water
   E) All of the above are inelastic

The correct answer is B:) Candy. Of the items on the list, candy is the one that a person is least likely to buy if it is too expensive.

70) What is the first step in the process of decision making of a purchase?

    A) Shopping around
    B) Recommendations
    C) Purchase evaluation
    D) Research
    E) Need awareness

The correct answer is E:) Need awareness.

71) If a product has a wholesale price of $750 and the retail price is $1,000, what is the markup percentage?

    A) 20%
    B) 33%
    C) 50%
    D) 75%
    E) 100%

The correct answer is B:) 33%. The difference between the two is $250, which is 33% of $750.

72) Which of the following is NOT a part of the Promotion marketing mix?

    A) Advertising
    B) Personal selling
    C) Sales promotion
    D) Publicity
    E) None of the above

The correct answer is E:) None of the above. Advertising, personal selling, sales promotion, and publicity are the four parts of the promotion marketing mix.

73) Marketing geared toward people with similar interests would be considered

    A) Demographic segmentation
    B) Geographic segmentation
    C) Psychographic segmentation
    D) Behavioral segmentation
    E) None of the above

The correct answer is C:) Psychographic segmentation. Psychographic segments are segments with similar lifestyles. These are groups of people with similar activities, values, interests, personalities and opinions.

74) When a company compares their performance to another's it is called

   A) Benchmarking
   B) Competitive advantage
   C) Diversification
   D) Differentiation
   E) Market share report

The correct answer is A:) Benchmarking. Benchmarking is the process of comparing a company's performance to that of another company, sometimes in the same industry or sector.

75) Which of the following presidents became known as a "trustbuster" for his use of the Sherman Antitrust Act?

   A) Harry Truman
   B) Theodore Roosevelt
   C) William Howard Taft
   D) Franklin D Roosevelt
   E) Grover Cleveland

The correct answer is B:) Theodore Roosevelt. Although the act was passed nearly ten years before his presidency, Roosevelt was the first to really use it to work against monopolies.

76) Which of the following is not a part of the SMART approach to creating objectives?

   A) Specific
   B) Measurable
   C) Achievable
   D) Realistic
   E) None of the above

The correct answer is E:) None of the above. The acronym SMART is used to create objectives that will be of the most benefit to the company. SMART stands for Specific, Measurable, Achievable, Realistic, and Timed.

77) The selling style of door to door salesmen is best classified as

    A) Relationship
    B) Technological
    C) Demographical
    D) Missionary
    E) None of the above

The correct answer is D:) Missionary. Missionary selling involves seeking out new customers and convincing them to buy the product for the first time.

78) A company that specializes in Halloween costumes and merchandise would have what type of a sales cycle?

    A) Upward moving trend
    B) Seasonal
    C) Flat line
    D) Stagnant
    E) None of the above

The correct answer is B:) Seasonal. Seasonal or cyclical sales patterns are typically regular and easy to predict.

79) Cognitive dissonance is also called

    A) Advocacy advertising
    B) Disposable income
    C) Buyer's remorse
    D) Inelastic demand
    E) Either A or C

The correct answer is C:) Buyer's remorse.

80) Which of the following is NOT a part of AOSTC?

    A) Analysis
    B) Objectives
    C) Strategies
    D) Tests
    E) Controls

The correct answer is D:) Tests.

81) Which of the following is an example of indirect advertising?

    A) Newspaper ads
    B) Internet ads
    C) TV commercials
    D) Word of mouth advertising
    E) Both B and D

The correct answer is D:) Word of mouth advertising. Word of mouth advertising isn't a direct advertisement of the company so it is indirect advertising.

82) The T is SWOT analysis stands for what?

    A) Testimonials
    B) Threats
    C) Territory
    D) Transformation
    E) None of the above

The correct answer is B:) Threats.

83) A college student working a part time job makes $800 a month after taxes. They have to pay $300 on their dorm (which includes utilities) and they have a meal plan that costs $130 a month. Their tuition has been broken down into monthly payments of $250. They have set aside $20 a month to go to the movies. What is their discretionary income?

    A) $800
    B) $500
    C) $120
    D) $100
    E) Cannot be determined without more information

The correct answer is C:) $120. There are no savings mentioned and cost of living includes the dorm costs, meal plan and tuition because these are the costs the student must pay. The movies fall under discretionary income and don't need to be considered in the calculations.

84) Because buyer's attitudes do not change very quickly, which of the following would be the best way to increase product awareness of a low fat butter?

   A) Grocery store demonstrations
   B) Coupons in the newspaper
   C) Television advertising
   D) Product placement
   E) All of the above

The correct answer is E:) All of the above. The more experienced a customer is with a name or a brand, the more likely they are to try it or buy it.

85) Which of the following is most likely an industrial product?

   A) Sports cars
   B) Board games
   C) Sugar
   D) Steel
   E) All of the above are consumer goods

The correct answer is D:) Steel. Of the items listed, steel is the least likely to be bought for personal use and the most likely to be bought for the manufacture of other items.

86) When a mixer is sold a three different major retail chains but each store has the identical pricing, it is easy to assume that the product is _____ by the manufacturer.

   A) Price fixing
   B) Price controlled
   C) Price differentiation
   D) Price discrimination
   E) None of the above

The correct answer is B:) Price controlled. Many products have a suggested MSRP (manufacturer's suggested retail price) while others have a MAP (minimum advertised price). MSRP is a suggestion while MAP is many times tied to a contract. Game system manufacturer's and audio electronics companies are a great example of MAP.

87) Which of the following BEST describes a cash cow product?

    A) High market growth and high relative market share
    B) High market growth and low relative market share
    C) Low market growth and high relative market share
    D) Low market growth and low relative market share
    E) None of the above

The correct answer is C:) Low market growth and high relative market share. In other words, it is one of the most recognized products in a field that doesn't sustain much change.

88) The CEO of a major corporation giving a talk show interview is an example of

    A) Advertising
    B) Goodwill
    C) Public relations
    D) Revenue generating
    E) None of the above

The correct answer is C:) Public relations.

89) If a product has a markup of $50 and the wholesale price is $100. What is the markup percentage?

    A) 10%
    B) 40%
    C) 50%
    D) 60%
    E) 70%

The correct answer is C:) 50%. 50 is 50% of 100.

90) Handling objections is part of

    A) Personal selling
    B) Advertising
    C) Marketing mix
    D) The four p's
    E) AOSTC

The correct answer is A:) Personal selling. Personal selling uses a five step process. It begins when a sales person (1) identifies a lead by prospecting, (2) makes a call or sends a letter to their prospect, (3) makes sales call/presentation, (4) handles any objectives by the customer and then (5) closes the sale. Personal selling is used in areas where the product is expensive, complicated or the price is negotiable. Examples include office copying systems, some insurance plans, high-end medical instruments, etc.

91) Which of the following is NOT true of the Federal Trade Commission Act?

    A) It created the Federal Trade Commission.
    B) It prevents unfair business practices.
    C) It gives the government the right to issue cease and desist orders.
    D) It prevents deceptive business practices.
    E) It made illegal any contract, deal, conspiracy or scheme to restrain trade.

The correct answer is E:) It made illegal any contract, deal, conspiracy or scheme to restrain trade. This was done by the Sherman Antitrust Act.

92) Which of the following is NOT a marketing control?

    A) Sales channel
    B) Market analysis
    C) Budgeting
    D) Cash flow statements
    E) Market research

The correct answer is A:) Sales channel. Market analysis, budgeting, cash flow statements and market research are all a part of marketing control.

93) Which of the following describes a dog product?

   A) High market growth and high relative market share
   B) High market growth and low relative market share
   C) Low market growth and high relative market share
   D) Low market growth and low relative market share
   E) None of the above

The correct answer is D:) Low market growth and low relative market share. It is a product in a slowly growing industry with little recognition. Financially speaking, they are worthless assets.

94) A decline in purchasing power due to price levels rising faster than income is called

   A) Price elasticity
   B) Balance of trade
   C) Market share penetration
   D) Inflation
   E) None of the above

The correct answer is D:) Inflation.

95) Which of the following acts amended the Clayton Act?

   A) Sherman Antitrust Act
   B) Clayton Act
   C) Robinson-Patman Act
   D) Federal Trade Commission Act
   E) North American Free Trade Agreement

The correct answer is C:) Robinson-Patman Act. The act expanded the Clayton Act to include not only local price cuts, but other forms of price discrimination as well.

96) Typically, who is the dominant member of the household responsible for selecting food items?

   A) Husband
   B) Wife
   C) Children
   D) Both husband and wife
   E) The entire family

The correct answer is B:) Wife. Typically, the wife is responsible for selecting food items, kitchenware, kitchen appliances, etc.

97) Which of the following acts gave the government the authority to issue cease and desist orders to companies using unfair or deceptive business practices?

   A) Sherman Antitrust Act
   B) Clayton Act
   C) Robinson-Patman Act
   D) Federal Trade Commission Act
   E) North American Free Trade Agreement

The correct answer is D:) Federal Trade Commission Act. The act was designed to prevent deceptive and unfair business practices and the FTC was created to do that.

98) Which of the following BEST describes push strategy promotion?

   A) Bringing the product to the consumer.
   B) Bringing the consumer to the product.
   C) Creating a demand for the product so that the consumer will seek it through their local stores.
   D) Pushing the product over so that someone will pick it up and possibly buy it.
   E) Both A and C

The correct answer is A:) Bringing the product to the consumer. The idea of push strategy is essentially putting the product somewhere that people are most likely to become aware of it and immediately buy it. Answers B and C describe pull strategy.

99) Segmentation based on gender would be classified as

    A) Demographic
    B) Geographic
    C) Psychographic
    D) Behavioral
    E) None of the above

The correct answer is A:) Demographic. Demographic segments are related to classifications of people within a population. This includes people with similar age, family situation, ethnicity, gender, jobs, income or religion.

100) A change in the average age of a population would be considered what type of change?

    A) Social
    B) Economic
    C) Technological
    D) Political
    E) Legal

The correct answer is A:) Social. Social changes are changes which relate to behavior and lifestyle.

Test Taking Strategies

Here are some test-taking strategies that are specific to this test and to other CLEP tests in general:

- Keep your eyes on the time. Pay attention to how much time you have left.
- Read the entire question and read all the answers. Many questions are not as hard to answer as they may seem. Sometimes, a difficult sounding question really only is asking you how to read an accompanying chart. Chart and graph questions are on most CLEP tests and should be an easy free point.
- If you don't know the answer immediately, the new computer-based testing lets you mark questions and come back to them later if you have time.
- Read the wording carefully. Some words can give you hints to the right answer. There are no exceptions to an answer when there are words in the question such as always, all or none. If one of the answer choices includes most or some of the right answers, but not all, then that is not the correct answer. Here is an example:

  The primary colors include all of the following:

  A) Red, Yellow, Blue, Green
  B) Red, Green, Yellow
  C) Red, Orange, Yellow
  D) Red, Yellow, Blue
  E) None of the above

  Although item A includes all the right answers, it also includes an incorrect answer, making it incorrect. If you didn't read it carefully, were in a hurry, or didn't know the material well, you might fall for this.

- Make a guess on a question that you do not know the answer to. There is no penalty for an incorrect answer. Eliminate the answer choices that you know are incorrect. For example, this will let your guess be a 1 in 3 chance instead.

What Your Score Means

Based on your score, you may, or may not, qualify for credit at your specific institution. At University of Phoenix, a score of 50 is passing for full credit. At Utah Valley University, the score is unpublished, the school will accept credit on a case-by-case basis. Another school, Brigham Young University (BYU) does not accept CLEP credit. To find out what score you need for credit, you need to get that information from your school's website or academic advisor.

You can score between 20 and 80 on any CLEP test. Some exams include percentile ranks. Each correct answer is worth one point. You lose no points for unanswered or incorrect questions.

Test Preparation

How much you need to study depends on your knowledge of a subject area. If you are interested in literature, took it in school, or enjoy reading then your studying and preparation for the literature or humanities test will not need to be as intensive as someone who is new to literature.

This book is much different than the regular CLEP study guides. This book actually teaches you the information that you need to know to pass the test. If you are particularly interested in an area, or you want more information, do a quick search online. We've tried not to include too much depth in areas that are not as essential on the test. Everything in this book will be on the test. It is important to understand all major theories and concepts listed in the table of contents. It is also very important to know any bolded words.

Don't worry if you do not understand or know a lot about the area. With minimal study, you can complete and pass the test.

One of the fallacies of other test books is test questions. People assume that the **content** of the questions are similar to what will be on the test. **That is not the case.** They are only to test your "test taking skills" so for those who know to read a question carefully, there is not much added value from taking a "fake" test.

To prepare for the test, make a series of goals. Allot a certain amount of time to review the information you have already studied and to learn additional material. Take notes as you study, as it will help you learn the material.

Legal Note

supported by or affiliated with the College Board, creators of the CLEP test. CLEP is a registered trademark of the College Entrance Examination Board, which does not endorse this book.

References

[1] *Adapted from Richard P. Coleman "The continuing significance of social class to marketing." "Journal of Consumer Research, December 1983, pp.265-80."*

[2] *Source: William D. Wells & George Gubar. "Life Cycle Concepts in Marketing Research," Journal of Marketing Research, Nov. 1996, pp. 355-63)*

FLASHCARDS

This section contains flashcards for you to use to further your understanding of the material and test yourself on important concepts, names or dates. You can cut these out to study from or keep them in the study guide, flipping the page over to check yourself.

Demand

What are the four P's?

Marketing Mix

Four Macro Economic Factors

Disposable Income

Components of Product Mix

Components of Price Mix

Components of Place Mix

Product, Price, Place Promotion

The need or want for a certain product

(1) Prosperity (also known as boom). (2) Recession (it is a slow down of business).
(3) Depression (gloom also called bust stage), and (4) Recovery (the economic upswing).

A company's products and promotions

Product line, quality, packaging, branding

Income that is earned but not set aside for a specific need - spending money

Logistics, sales territories, types of channels, market location

Basic price, transport, credit terms

Components of Promotion Mix

Durable Goods

Non-durable Goods

Services

Convenient Goods

Shopping Goods

Specialty Goods

Self-actualization

These tangible goods (actual goods), which once bought will satisfy you for many years. (Example: Air Conditioners, Refrigerators, Clothing, etc).

Advertising, Publicity, Personal Selling, Sales Promotion

These non-tangible activities, benefits and satisfactions that are offered by individuals with expertise. (Example: Tailoring, Hair dressing, Cleaning, General Repairing etc).

These are also tangible goods which once bought may be consumed in a very short period of time. (Example: Toothpaste, Soap, Ham, biscuits, etc).

Goods bought by consumers after spending time on its utility, value, quality, suitability, style and of course, price. (Example: Cars, Home appliances. Dress materials, Furniture, etc).

Goods bought by consumers most often with relative speed without spending time on comparison. (Example: Newspapers, soaps, detergents, tobacco products, etc).

Highest need in Maslow's hierarchy of needs - Level 5

Goods bought by consumers that have characteristics perceived to be unique and/or having good brand identification. (Example: Branded goods, fancy goods, electronic goods, photographic equipment etc).

Esteem Needs

Belonging and Love

Safety

Physical Needs

Caste

Social Class

Reference Groups

Face to Face Groups

Level 3 need

Level 4 need

Level 1 need

Level 2 need

Identifies members on the basis of (superior or inferior) positions held by them

Aspirations of members is largely in keeping with the known and traditionally followed systems and practices

These are groups which have direct and immediate influence on a person's opinions, likes and dislikes. Example: The person's family, friends, neighbors, peers etc.

A person may not be a member of such groups but identifies with it and aspires to become one - such groups are known as reference groups

Family

Biogenic Needs

Psychogenic Needs

Examples of Demographic Segmentation

Extended Product

Four Stages of the Product Lifecycle

Sales Channel

In the four P's, what is place referred to?

Concerned with your physiological state. Example: Hunger, thirst, discomfort, etc.

A persons basic attitudes, behaviors and beliefs are during the formative years, formed through interaction with his family, which plays a most enduring role in such attitude formation

Sex, age, status

A persons specific need satisfaction relating to his psychological state of mind, which normally is not apparent. Example: Satisfying need for recognition, esteem, etc.

Introduction, Growth, Maturity, Decline

Tangible products - together with a gamut of service going with the products

How or where customers get your product

Through who a good is sold until it reaches the consumer

Federal Trade Commission

Cartel

Direct marketing

Indirect marketing

Star

Cash cow

Problem child

Dog

A group of distinct firms that work together essentially creating a monopoly.

A five person, bipartisan board created by the Federal Trade Commission Act.

A more neutral approach to advertising which includes word of mouth advertising or recognition through participation in the community.

A hands on approach to marketing which includes telemarketing and advertisements.

A product with a high market share in a slow growing industry.

A product with a high market share in a fast growing industry.

A product with low market growth and low relative market share.

A product with a low relative market share in a fast growing market.

Advocacy advertising

Clayton Act

Question mark

Buyer's remorse

Pull promotion

Push promotion

Legal changes

Economic changes

Amendment to Sherman Antitrust Act which specifically mentioned local price cuts and exclusive sales contracts.

Advertising which is designed to support one side of a controversial issue.

Another name for cognitive dissonance.

Another name for a problem child.

Bringing the product to the consumer and making sure they know about it.

Bringing the consumer to the product and creating a demand for it.

Changes in the state of the economy, inflation, interest rates and average wages are also economic changes.

Changes in laws which affect how business function.

Political changes

Social changes

Discretionary income

Heterogeneous

Robinson-Patman Act

Psychographic segments

Technological changes

Inelastic demand

Changes which relate to
behavior and lifestyle.

Changes on a worldwide
level which effect trade.

Diverse or varied
products.

Discretionary income is
income that is left over
after a person has paid
for basic necessities.

Groups of people with
similar activities, values,
interests, personalities
and opinions.

Expanded Clayton Act to
include all forms of price
discrimination.

Inelastic products are
products that people will
buy no matter what the
cost.

Increases and
advancements in
technology which
change how people
consider the market.

Missionary selling

Sherman Antitrust Act

Homogeneous

Market growth rate

Markup

Industrial Products

Disposable income

NAFTA

Made it illegal for any contract, deal, conspiracy or scheme to restrain trade.

Involves seeking out new customers and convincing them to buy the product for the first time.

Market growth rate is how quickly the particular market is growing for a product.

Manufactured to be all the same.

Meant to be bought by companies and used to produce other products.

Markup is the difference between the actual price of the product to the store and the price they sell the product for.

North American Free Trade Agreement. Established free trade among Canada, the United States and Mexico.

Net income after taxes.

Monopoly

Demographic segments

Federal Trade Commision Act

Elastic demand

Relative market share

Geographic segments

Behavioral segments

Tariff

People with similar age, family situation, ethnicity, gender, jobs, income, religion.

One company is the sole manufacturer of a product and there is no close substitute.

Products for which the demand varies greatly dependent on price.

Prevents companies from using unfair or deceptive business practices.

Segmentation based on location.

Relative market share is how prominent the product is within the market.

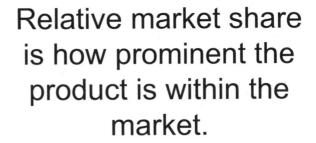

Tariffs are taxes levied on goods imported from (or exported to) another country.

Segmentation based on people's attitude toward the product.

Relationship selling

Wholesale price

Retail price

Consumer products

Cognitive dissonance

Vertical channels

Herizontal channels

Break even

The price which the store receives the product for.

The idea is to start a genuine relationship with the client, to listen to their needs and concerns, so that they will keep coming back.

Typically purchased in retail stores for personal or household use.

The price which the store sells the product for.

When all the levels of production and distribution for a product are owned by the same person.

When a person has second thoughts about whether they purchased the correct product.

Where total revenue equals total cost (fixed and variable expenses).

When companies on the same level of production team up.